A Chance to

Forgiving those who are not sorry

By Nel Bennet

God bless you
ᴗ Nel ✗ 2021

a chance to be sorry @ hotmail.com

A Chance to be Sorry

Copyright etc

Book production, cover design and print by Halcyon, via NB Publishing.

Further copies for sale at several retailers and at

www.scripturegifts.co.uk

Contact Nel via www.facebook.com/a chance to be sorry

ACKNOWLEDGEMENTS

Thank you to:

God: for his many, many blessings.

Family: My husband, our children and their partners for their support; my sister and her children for standing with me and her husband for his outrage about our treatment.

Friends: My church and non-church friends for walking with me in the good and the difficult times.

Church: All the leadership, the teams and the members.

Listeners: Joy, Michelle, Katie, Elaine, Lena, Polly and Steve

Doctor: Caroline for hearing and responding to my needs physically and psychologically.

Supporters: Terry and Dave for their reassuring support.

Prayer: Sheila -The Immanuel Approach Prayer Ministry.

Proof readers: Elizabeth, Helen R, Terry, Tony, Lois & Liam; Sarah, Sandra, Georgina, Pauline, Ross & Lucy; Jennie, Wendy, Phil, Jo, Margaret, Susanna, Sheila & Malcolm.

IT: Jo for helping me with technical and media things.

Christian retreat: Clare and Peter for my place to write.

Launch: Helen K for helping me to launch this book.

The Police and Crown Prosecution Services for pursuing justice.

A Chance to be Sorry

Forgiving those who are not sorry

Forgiving those who are sorry for hurting you is one thing but what about forgiving those who are not sorry and who blame you for your own pain... and for theirs?

Nel tells her story of surviving abuse in childhood, of finding comfort in her Christian faith and of eventually finding the courage, in her forties, to confront her abuser via the legal system.

Nel's story offers insight into the wide-reaching effects of abuse, into reporting an abuser and around how she finds strength, through her Christian faith, to forgive those who are sorry and those who are not sorry for their part in it all.

This is a book of two-parts. In the first part Nel tells her story, sparing the reader the explicit details.

In the second part Nel shares her research and the understanding this has given her, which includes a list of resources and contacts for help.

 Victims of abuse are often called survivors, having survived a terrible crime. Both terms are used in this book. Some survivors prefer to be called 'thrivers' but to avoid confusion just two descriptions are used.

10% of the author's profits from this book will go to NSPCC's Childline (National Society for the Prevention of Cruelty to Children) and 10% will go to NAPAC (The National Association for People Abused in Childhood).

CONTENTS:

Trigger warning

Traumas recalled (mainly in Chapters 2 and 3), may trigger flashbacks in other survivors.

"People need their experiences to be acknowledged as authentic."

Archbishop Desmond Tutu [Ref 0.1]

INTRODUCTION:

No one wants it to be true but, statistically, most people reading this book will know someone who has suffered abuse of some kind; sadly, many readers will have experienced abuse themselves. *Ref 0.2*

For nearly forty years I felt I had to keep quiet about the physical, mental and sexual abuse I had suffered, for fear of reprisals from the perpetrator and for fear of bringing shame on the family.

Writing this book gives me some acknowledgment of my experience. In recent years speaking to counsellors and to friends and reporting the crime to the police offered me acknowledgement too.

Some reading this book will never have had any acknowledgement. They may not have been listened to and many may have had the crimes against them minimised.

I know my experience will be different from other survivors' experiences but my hope is that they will all find some comfort in reading this book. Some may have been persuaded to be compliant with the abuse, some may have felt able to fight it and some may have done both. Some may have felt unable to report the crime against them (as I did for nearly forty years) and some may have reported it to the police. During my childhood I thought everyone else had happy families and it was just us suffering. I want to try to help release other survivors from feeling alone and encourage them to secure support. I hope those who have not been victims of abuse will gain some understanding of the enormity of this crime and how it affects survivors, their families, their friends and society as a whole and how child abuse can be 'hidden in plain sight,' as the consequences of this crime are suffered by more than **one-in-seven adults**. [Ref 0.2and 0.3]

I have spared the reader the explicit details of my experience, whilst giving an authentic account. I have tried to be sensitive to my siblings without diluting the effects of abuse and betrayal. My sister Zoe has her own story to tell, so I have not gone into detail about her experience. Zoe has given this book her blessing.

My many proof-readers are from various professions including the police, social services, education and the field of psychotherapy. Some are Christians and some are not.

My current day-to-day life is good; my cup runs over. I only bring my story out now to shed light on this crime in order to try to help others.

References

0.1 Tutu, Desmond, referring to South African Truth& Reconciliation, (1996). Tutu was Chair of this Commission, which was set up to look into human rights violations around apartheid. Tutu is also the author of several books on forgiveness.

0:2 NSPCC cites L Radford, etal, 'Child Abuse and Neglect in the UK Today' (2011) estimates there are 11 million adult survivors of child sexual abuse of some kind in the UK and that this crime costs the UK £3.2 billion a year. UK population is over 66 million [Ref 0.3] *www.nspcc.org*

0.3 Office of National Statistics Source dataset: Population estimates time series dataset (pop). (2018). www.ons.gov.uk

*"Give me a child to the age of seven
and I will show you the wo/man."*

Aristotle [Ref 1.1]

My story – to the Age of Seven - Chapter 1
Favourite Things

(Mum and Dad recounted their part of my story to me over the years).

In his mid-twenties Dad was a jazz-loving, photographer for the city's newspaper and Mum was a pretty, young, reporter for the same paper. They became friends whilst covering jazz events in the late 1950's. This progressed to a whirlwind romance, which included lots of dancing, walks along the riverbank and sharing a bathtub, which led to a surprise conception.

Marriage and the birth of my sister, Zoe, dampened the glamour but the romance continued and I was on the way within two years.

In the summer of 1961, just before I was born, Dad took the photographs for the paper's feature story and a man called Wayne was pictured at his workplace as part of this. Dad and Mum became friends with Wayne, his wife and their young children. They socialised as families and partied as couples. Wayne and Mum flirted with each other and after I was born, they met up a few times. It was at a Christmas party in 1961 that they began their affair fully.

The following spring Mum left two-year-old Zoe and six-month-old me, to be with Wayne, who left his wife and children. Dad was heartbroken. Both marriages were in ruins.

Divorce and custody battles were fought vehemently in the courts but, unusually for the 1960s, the judge granted Dad custody of Zoe and me, with our Nan as his support.

In December 1964 Dad bought a new house in another city and we moved there with Nan. Dad then worked as a freelance photographer. We never met our Grandfather, who apparently lived abroad.

Forty miles away, Mum and Wayne bought a farmhouse, with land, in the countryside and lived there with a new baby, Gary. By the end of 1964 they had three children and had set their home up as a small hotel.

Zoe and I had a wonderful early childhood with Nan and Dad. Dad was fun and affectionate but sometimes he seemed sad. He was slim with dark hair, straight teeth and smiley eyes. He was out at work a lot, as most dads were.

Although only in her fifties Nan had short, white, wiry hair and dressed in old-fashioned skirts and tops with thick tights, flat shoes and a pinny. Her twinkly blue eyes shone with mischief from her powdered-pink face with its false-teeth smile. She was a sunny sort of person who was lots of fun.

Nan had served in the war but not in any kitchens and her cooking was terrible. Burnt spam fritters were served up regularly. Dad showed us how to make beans on toast at a very young age, so we could eat something vaguely healthy when he was out. But I do have fond memories of watching 'The Wooden Tops' (a 1960s children's television programme) on our black and white TV, in front of the gas fire, drinking sweet tea and eating digestive biscuits with Nan.

Our summers seemed to smell of tarmac melting in the heat mingled with the aroma of the rose petal perfume we made and tried to sell at the garden gate. We had a gang of friends who we played marbles and hopscotch with; we played kiss-catch in the park, hide-and-seek in the graveyard and Chinese-skipping with long pieces of elastic, in the playground. We spent hours perfecting hand-stands, cartwheels and head-over-heels then held roly-poly races down an embankment.

We spent a lot of time at the local swimming baths. Nan told us we could not go swimming on a particular day but we went anyway. Nan's legs appeared at the window by the pool, like the mother's legs in the Tom & Jerry cartoon. She was very cross with us. These same legs appeared when I broke an ornament and hid under the table. Nan could be stern as well as sunny.

Brown paper packages tied up with string regularly arrived for Zoe and me, containing matching outfits hand knitted by kind great-aunts. Red cable-knit skirts were a favourite.

Big black taxi cabs took us to the train station to go on trips to visit these great aunties and uncles and Dad's cousins. Their kindness when we visited them was wonderful. Being chosen to be bridesmaids at cousin Jane's wedding was such a treat. Our long satin dresses, in rich dark green, were finished off with matching pillbox hats covered with white flowers and we carried white posies.

We went to a very modern city infant school, which was bright and airy with big windows, large corridors and a huge central hall. We had new black patent shoes and smocked dresses for the school Christmas party and took part in nativity plays with Dad taking photographs of all the children. We went carol singing around the neighbourhood with a group of five to eight-year olds and were given pocket money; just a few of my favourite things that were part of my early childhood.

On winter days Nan nodded off whilst we played. One day, as she slept, we made her face up like a clown. When someone came to the door and she woke up and answered it in full clown makeup, we laughed uncontrollably.

Dad despaired at Nan at times. Like the time she left a boiled kettle on the floor and I bounded off the sofa hooking the kettle with my foot and pouring hot water down my leg. Dad wrapped me in his duffle coat and ran all the way to the doctor's surgery down the road. No scars thankfully.

Dad made us believe we were the brightest and most beautiful children ever born. Zoe did win a baby competition but I was a bit more mischievous looking!

Dad often took us with him on his photo shoots. Gymkhanas were a regular weekend earner. Dad took photographs of the horses and their riders going over the jumps, then developed mini-proofs of the pictures in the back of his van and set these up on a board for people to order full-sized prints from. Royalty were at some of these events. Dad showed me how to take the orders not long after I had learnt to write. At the end of the day the three of us rode home in the front of his van. Family portraits taken in people's homes were also popular and lucrative. Dad sometimes let us help him with the orders in his dark room, which was also his bedroom. He had it completely blacked-out, to enable him to develop the film reels, though it often had a faint orange glow about it. Dad enlarged the photographs on to paper on a big grey machine. I was entranced by the sight of the images emerging as he carefully dipped this paper in large plastic trays of chemicals, before rinsing them and pegging them up to dry. The acidic smell of these chemicals seemed to linger throughout our home.

We never tired of seeing Dad's photographs in daylight, then watching him post them off to customers. Dad was often melancholy though and he would then disappear into his darkroom to work alone for hours. Other times he came home with unusual gifts like the pink paper dresses and pants he bought us (I don't think the former caught on but the latter are still used in hospitals). He took us to markets and warehouses and treated us to Barbie-type dolls, which we played with for hours. He bought us a colour projector which we used under the dining room table to show slides on the wall of Snow White and the Seven Dwarves. The colours were so vivid that I could almost taste the apple!

Dad sometimes whisked us out on surprise trips, once singing: "How much is that doggie in the window, the one with the waggly tail," as he drove us to a pet shop where he bought us our puppy, who we named 'Fred.' Fred smelt of biscuits and was soft and round. His tan colour fur was punctuated by black eye brows and a short black beard. We carried him around like a baby and played with him until he fell asleep in front of the fire.

Dad sang to us when he put us to bed. 'The Little White Cloud that Cried,' [Ref 1.0] was a regular bedtime song. Such was his repertoire about

Santa Claus that one Christmas Eve I actually saw Santa's sleigh, just briefly. When I found the red scooter at the end of my bed in the morning I was convinced. Zoe later enlightened me that he was: "Just Dad in his duffle coat." Zoe taught me so many things, including how to ride a bike at quite a young age so that I could join our gang of friends on the long bike rides they planned.

One summer Dad took us to a seaside resort in his van and left us at a seafront hotel, with Nan, whilst he went back home to work. We caught tiny fish from the sea with our fishing nets, put them in sea water in our small buckets and took them into our hotel room. The three of us walked along the promenade in the evenings, breathing in the salty air and looking at the gardens, which were lit by colourful Disney-type characters.

When I was seven-years-old, a gang of us cycled 18 miles or so to another town. We had some idea that our other grandparents lived there, though we didn't know where. We bought milk shakes and explored.

On the way home, when another child's bike had a puncture, we called off at a house and asked for a bowl of water so we could repair it. The couple gave us all a drink too. There was no fear of strangers then. We had such a good time we went to the same town again a few weeks later. We had ballet and tap lessons and performed in several shows. Zoe and I were Bonnie & Clyde in one of these. We wore bright orange polyester bell bottom trousers in another show and sequins were patiently sewn on to our dresses by Nan for another.

Regular ice-skating trips saw us skating forwards and backwards at a young age, which was lots of fun. Birthday parties with our friends playing games and eating sandwiches and jelly, with a special cake from the bakery, were very much enjoyed. I have fond memories of brownies and Sunday school; of going to the theatre to see Harry Worth and to the cinema to see The Sound of Music.

Dad loved his jazz music but the record that I remember him playing the most was Mary Hopkins singing: 'Those Were the Days my Friends,' *(Ref.12)* and for us they certainly were as what happened next led to their untimely end.

"Would you like to visit your mummy?" Nan asked. This came out of the blue when I was about seven-years-old. I had only recently become aware that I had or hadn't got a mum. Dad had not allowed any photographs of her in the house.

The subject came up a few times and being adventurous, spirited children, we went along with it. Mum had secured access visits. This meant we were to go out for the day with her and her new family.

I was excited and quite scared when a big, black, bulbous car pulled up outside our house one day and Nan ushered Zoe and me towards it. Dad stayed indoors with the curtains closed. I got in the back of the car and sat behind our new stepfather. His large frame spilled over the driver's seat and his trilby hat touched the roof of the car. I noticed his broad, pink, pimply neck. My heart was pounding so much I thought it would come through my cardigan.

19

My eyes quickly turned to the two young boys sharing the front seat. Both had black leather-type bomber-jackets on. Gary had dark curly hair and David had straight brown hair framing a very round face. I decided I was probably a bit like David as the rest of them, like Zoe, had dark, almost black hair.

Mum sat in the back with Zoe, Trish and me. Trish was nearly three and her dark curly hair sat on the white collar of her red velvet dress. I looked up at my new mum, who had her hair up in a bun on the top of her head. My eyes were the same colour as hers. I wondered if my teeth would protrude, like her top teeth, when I grew up. I practiced sitting them on my bottom lip. When she took a tissue from her handbag I wondered if she was crying and I thought that might be a good thing, but she just blew her nose. Our new brothers and sister seemed as bemused as we were.

They took us to see our new grandma and grandad in the next town. They lived quite near the milkshake shop we had visited on our bike rides. Grandma could cook and she had made us some treats to eat, but she couldn't speak much. We were told that she had a stroke when our parents split up. She was very ladylike in every way except that when she got frustrated about not being able to speak, she just swore, which we all found quite funny.

We were also told that Wayne had his own children but that he didn't see them as they lived a long way away but he made a point of telling us that he paid towards their upbringing.

Day visits led to weekend trips. Mum and Wayne had a small-holding in the countryside with land and lots of animals. They had renovated the farmhouse and turned it into a small hotel. It had an open fire at one end and an Aga-type, multi-fuel range cooker at the other.

They took us horse riding on one of our weekend visits and I loved it. Eventually we were invited to go for Whit week (the May school holiday). This sounded wonderful to me and with the promise of more horse riding the prospect of that week felt like a dream. And it was.

But our dad was suffering. Every time they came to collect us, he either went out or shut all the curtains. His melancholy was tangible at these pickups and his mood dropped over the months. One evening he argued with Nan about this and became so upset that he punched the wall and his fist made a hole in it.

I woke another morning to be told that Dad had been taken away to hospital in the night, after becoming extremely distressed. I had slept through it. When he returned home, he was sad and loving.

After our next weekend stay with Mum, as we were about to leave, Zoe told Mum about Dad's hospital visit. I stood behind her as her words tumbled out and everything inside me cried out:

"No, no, no!" But the words were out. They asked us lots of questions then Mum said we would not be allowed to live with Dad and Nan, ever. I felt so stunned I didn't even cry, although I was desperately sad inside.

We never went back to our home again and we were not even allowed to speak to or see Dad or Nan at all. This felt like a constant loss, a sort of ache, which I put to the back of my mind, throughout my upbringing.

References

1.0 Johnnie Ray 1951; The Little White Cloud That Cried song.

1.1 Aristotle, Greek Philosopher 384-322 BC ('wo/' my own edit).

1.2 'Those were the Days,' (Raskin G 1968) sung by Mary Hopkins

"Rough winds do shake the darling

buds of May."

William Shakespeare [Ref 2.1]

My Story – Mid Childhood -Chapter 2

Darling Buds

1969 saw the first man land on the moon and it saw us taken by bus to a small village primary school in a Victorian building in the middle of the countryside. Its main hall was the same size as the corridor at our old school. The windows were set up high, which made the school feel small and dark. The kindness of the teachers who welcomed us there in the middle of that summer term made the move bearable though.

Mum encouraged us to call Wayne 'Daddy' and she changed our surname to his. She told us we would be ashamed at school if we had a different surname to our parents and siblings.

The hotel and smallholding where we now lived must have seemed idyllic to visitors, and there were many of them, as Mum provided 'Teas-on-the-Lawn'. A large tree in the centre of the huge garden had a swing tied from its main branch with steps leading up its trunk to a treehouse, which we could exit down the slide on its other side. There was a rose bed, a row of apple trees, a vegetable patch; there were rabbits in hutches and pet goats. All added to the pretty family scene. We rescued kittens from being drowned by a local farmer, rode ponies and made dens in haystacks. We played badminton, cricket and football in the garden, for hours at a time.

In the early days Mum took us all on long walks through fields of cows and bullocks, avoiding the field with the big bull in it. We walked along the riverbank and arrived back home muddy and hungry. After washing our hands and feet, we all tucked into a stew, then sat by the fire. I liked being in a big family and having a mum and I very much enjoyed being in the countryside. I did miss Dad and Nan and our old gang of friends though.

When we were playing in the garden one day, a removal van pulled up outside the gate and our dog Fred jumped out and ran towards us. I was so happy to see him so I picked him up and hugged him as he licked my ears. Nan sat in the passenger seat in the front of the van. I longed to run to her but we were not allowed to speak to her. That ache surfaced and my eyes filled with tears.

A man (who turned out to be a social worker) brought some of our things in to the hotel. Zoe and I watched from a distance, bewildered. As they drove away, I felt very sad and confused.

In the early days we were occasionally allowed to write to Nan and Dad under Mum's supervision. She told us to write to tell our Dad that we now called Wayne 'Daddy' but we refused to do this.

They took us to see a solicitor and told us what to say to him. I can't remember the things happening that they told us to say; I can only remember telling the solicitor about them.

With two dogs and several cats already in the family we were not allowed to keep our dog, Fred. He was soon re-homed with one of Wayne's work colleagues, which made me sad. They persuaded us that it was the best option for him but it hurt to see Fred go.

Whenever the subject of our dad came up, they told us that he was dangerous. Mum gave me a big red purse with some money in it so that if he snatched us back, we should get a bus back to their local town and ring them. One day, when I was doing cartwheels in a field, I lost the purse and I felt relieved to have lost it.

We had lived with them for just a few weeks when Wayne first whacked me around the face. I remember feeling horrified that my mum did not come to my rescue and that there was no one to ask for help. We lived several miles from the town, with buses only running on a Saturday, other than school buses. Wayne was six feet tall, very muscular and weighed almost twenty stone and his violence reared its head regularly; from kicking David around the dining room like a football to bashing Mum's head on the wall.

One night I woke up feeling really ill and I ran to Mum's bedroom. Her door was locked, so I banged on it saying I felt ill and I needed her. She shouted:

"Go away!" I turned to go to the bathroom and was sick on the landing. "And you can clean that up!" She shouted. I cleaned it up, sorted myself out and went back to bed, feeling sad and unwanted.

I was eager to please Mum and Wayne by helping and I even baked him birthday cakes. I was one of the main cooks at home by the age of ten; with a big family and hotel guests there was a lot of cooking to be done! Sometimes as Mum sat on the sofa, we brushed her long hair over the back of it. Having had a Nan with white wiry hair this was quite a novelty.

Zoe and I babysat from a very young age and on Saturday nights we helped Mum with her makeup. She looked pretty with her hair in a high bun, wearing a black maxi skirt with a flouncy blouse and high heels. Meanwhile Wayne preened himself in the mirror, combing his greying, wispy hair over the top of his balding head from one side to the other. He then secured it by spraying lots of hairspray on it. This was followed by splashes of aftershave to his ruddy face and neck. Our Dad was a private man, who was clean shaven and always wore a suit and polished shoes. I never saw him in a vest or splashing aftershave or spraying hairspray; it was all very strange to me.

Whilst they were out, we went on a hunt for goodies. Tinned peaches were an easy steal; we'd burn the wrappers on the fire and bury the tins. I don't think we were badly fed overall, as we had a lot of stews and casseroles and plenty of vegetables, but treats were less frequent.

At one stage they ran a village tuck shop though and they hid the sweets under their bed. Zoe and I found them and ate a couple of cream eggs each. Later Trish took a walloping from Wayne for this. We felt guilty and later we told her so. She said:

"Don't worry; I ate loads!" She had been on the hunt for treats too!

When they were out, we watched 'Thriller' on the new colour TV (a 1970s drama where blood filled the screen at the beginning and the end whilst spooky music played) or 'Dracula', which was still in black and white. We sat on the sofa and hid under a blanket when the scary bits happened.

Later, when we heard their car pull up in the drive, we peeped through the gap in our bedroom curtains. On one occasion the outside lights lit the two couples lying down in the car and I remember puzzling why Mum's long legs were coming out of the driver's side window with another man's legs and Wayne's thick legs were coming out of the rear passenger window with another woman's short thin legs. Another time, when we peered through the keyhole of the office door, we saw Wayne kissing one of the members of staff. It was all very confusing.

When we first went to live with them, we went to Sunday school in the village church but before long Mum assigned us the job of cooking the Sunday dinner whilst they went to the pub. We waited tentatively to see what mood they were in when they came back. Sometimes they were happy, other times they fought or he started on one of us. Either way they fell asleep on the sofa after lunch. After clearing up we went out on our bikes to the nearest shop, about three miles away, to buy a bar of chocolate and a packet of mints.

Gary was often called names and taunted by Wayne but he never hit him. Mum protected him and Wayne knew that Gary was off limits, physically at least. I wished she would protect me too.

When we were told the news that Mum was having another baby it was the most wonderful moment. If it was a girl the boys planned to put her in the bin! If it was a girl though, Zoe and I would be allowed to choose her name. We had no hesitation and we chose her name there and then: 'Alison Jane', after our own Dad's two kind cousins. Mum kept contact with his aunts so she didn't object to this.

Winter evenings were cosy around the inglenook fireplace with its roaring fire. Numerous cats and two dogs stretched out and played on the rug, to everyone's amusement. Sunday nights were spent watching 1970s' series such as Poldark, then at other times: On the Buses, Morecambe and Wise and Benny Hill. Children's programmes such as The Banana Splits, Scooby Doo, The Rolf Harris Show (more on Rolf later) and other classic 1970s shows were very much enjoyed. Most memorable is the build up to Top of the Pops on a Thursday night.

Power cuts seemed to be a regular feature of life. The news on the television was often about people going on strike from their jobs and of shortages of food and power. We felt fortunate as we had an open fire and a multi-fuel range cooker to cook on and bake in, whilst some people were cold and some went hungry.

Christmases were accompanied by Slade and all those wonderful 1970s Christmas songs. One snowy December the hotel guests helped us build snowmen and one guest was particularly artistic giving his snowman full facial features. He also made us an igloo.

Christmas Days were mostly peaceful. In the early years we had presents at the end of our beds in pillowcases. These were sparse but always included a selection box and sometimes an annual such as 'Debbie'. Wayne cooked the dinner on Christmas Day and his cooking was better than our mum's.

The local Avon lady bought us all a present one Christmas and I can still remember how special it made me feel unwrapping this and having my very own 'Moonwind' talcum powder!

We played long games of Monopoly and Chess and very much enjoyed our Twister game. I clung on to these normal family moments.

Then came that lovely Spring morning, when I was ten-years-old. Zoe came into our bedroom, with Wayne, to tell me that 'Alison Jane' had been born in the night. Zoe leapt on to her top bunk bed full of all the details of our new sister. I was so excited.

Alison was a rosy child who looked very much like Wayne but we loved her even so.

Although Mum initially breast fed her, she was soon on formula milk, which in those days was given in a thick glass bottle with a rubber teat stretched over the end. I loved giving her a bottle and quickly learned to change her nappies and care for her.

Alison had a big coach pram and I pushed her around the garden in it planning how I could run away with her and look after her on my own. She spent little time crying as one of us always picked her up.

A locked box was put on the inside of the letterbox so we couldn't receive any letters without Wayne vetting them, but Mum did give us the pocket money Dad and Nan sent for Zoe and me. Then, one day when I was drying the pots and went to put these away one of Alison's glass bottles fell out of the cupboard and smashed on the floor. Mum took my pocket money off me to pay for this.

Mum told us that Dad had a new girlfriend and that they had just had a baby boy together. This news was both exciting and confusing for me. I thought perhaps our dad didn't need us or want us anymore. My heart ached for Dad and Nan.

Meanwhile Wayne had fallen out with Grandad so we didn't see him or Grandma for a few years; we missed them too.

Mum ran the businesses whilst Wayne went to his new job at the local hospital, working with mental health patients, then working with her on his days off. Running a small-holding and hotel all helped feed the large family and kept Zoe and me busy when we were not at school: loading the twin-tub washing machine, pegging-out washing, doing the ironing and so on. Mum referred to us as her right-hand men.

We earned pocket money and when I had saved enough, I went clothes shopping, but I struggled to choose things. I had a little 'puppy-fat' and Mum and Wayne had mocked me about this. On my first shopping trip I came back with random clothing and toiletries and from then on, I bought my own toiletries and clothes. Mum did buy my uniform for secondary school but I had to have this from the men's shop so it could be passed down to my brother. I really didn't mind as big collars were quite the fashion in the 1970s!

One day, when Wayne was at work and Mum was out, Zoe and I pushed the sofas back in the lounge, closed the curtains and set our record player up to play our new record. It was so exciting watching the new black vinyl single drop on to the turntable and the needle position itself on to this record. All five children danced around the room doing slow flying impressions to Fleetwood Mac's instrumental, 'Albatross,' [Ref 2.2] playing this over and over again.

Another day as we walked along the lane by the small caravan site in our village, we heard the six-year-old boy who lived there with his mum shout to us:

"We've got crazy horses in our caravan." We could hear the Ywow, ywow, of the guitar on this Osmonds' hit, 'Crazy Horses'. [Ref 2.3]

'Cracklin' Rosie' by Neil Diamond [Ref 2.4] rang out through the hotel when an older cousin came to stay. Although she was Wayne's niece, Eileen was kind and fun. We got on really well and she invited me to stay with her family a few times. I felt safe with them.

The summer when I was 12 years-old, Mum evicted all the children except for baby Alison into a mobile home in the garden to make room for more hotel guests. I quite liked having the end bedroom to myself. I felt special as I settled myself in. We had very few books but one I read over and over was called: 'I Wanted a Pony.' This was my dream as I loved horse riding. I lost myself in this book. I had been enjoying riding a neighbour's horse for them but was soon banned as it took me away from the hotel for too long, but I still dreamed of owning my own pony. That night I read for a short time, then fell asleep.

My dreams were interrupted by strange heavy breathing by my bed and I woke with a start. I could smell Wayne's aftershave. What was he doing in here? As I stirred, I realised he was abusing me. My heart raced so fast that I thought I might die. I held my breath and wanted to jump out of bed and run but I just froze. I didn't understand what was happening, I wanted to scream but nothing came out. I felt horrified and afraid. I remember eventually seeing his huge white-vested profile leaving my room. I don't think I cried, but I did feel desperate for someone to help me. I started to shake and felt empty, invaded and broken. Everything had changed. I felt ashamed I had let this happen to me. I have buried some memories about that night but I do remember being on the school bus the next day feeling sad and confused. I looked around at the other children. I was sure this wasn't right and that they weren't living with this so, as I looked out of the bus window at the distant fields, I promised myself that I would not let it happen again. I knew I would have to fight to protect myself. I insisted on moving into the mobile home's other bedroom that night, where I slept in the double bed with Zoe and Trish.

I dodged and dived to avoid Wayne and planned how I could make sure I was not alone with him. If he came near me, I made a lot of noise; coughing or anything to draw attention. I wasn't always successful and it repulses me to think of how he regularly tried to kiss me as I pushed his huge belly away.

"Give your dad a cuddle," was his lead in line. He was affectionate with Mum and all the children but I knew what would follow for me when they weren't around so I wriggled out of his grasp as quickly as possible. He then mocked me and implied that I was being difficult or unloving. I had had a loving relationship with my own Dad so I knew this wasn't true and I missed Nan and Dad even more at these times. I wondered what our life with them would have been like if we hadn't been snatched from them, but there seemed to be no way back.

When our school friends were going off to meet up after school, we had to go home on the school bus to peel huge pans of potatoes and do chores. I made friends at school but it was hard to build on these friendships as I was rarely able to meet up with them for out-of-school activities. It didn't help that Mum let me take Mondays and Fridays off to help her in the businesses. That was until the Deputy Head called me into her office and very gently pointed out that I was only doing 'a three-day-week' (a phrase coined in the strikes of the 1970s).

Academically I was in the top groups but this made things worse in a way. The others all seemed confident and secure and seemed to be from lovely, normal families. Even though they didn't know about my home life, I felt ashamed. I feared anyone finding out what he had done to me and what he was, believing that I would be ostracised.

One Saturday evening, after Zoe and I had looked after the children and the businesses all day (whilst our parents went out drinking), we were allowed to go out with a friend to a teen disco in the next town. Her older brother collected us in his car and dropped us off. We were excited and felt quite grown up walking towards the event. As we approached the entrance our parents' car pulled up alongside us. My heart sank.

"Get in!" Mum yelled at me.

"Why, what have I done?" I retaliated.

"Do as your mother tells you and get in now!" Wayne shouted. They didn't take Zoe, just me. I was furious. I had worked like a slave all day and could not think what it was they wanted me for.

"It's not fair!" I protested.

"Let me drive," Mum said.

Wayne got in the back of the car and proceeded to beat me up. I rolled myself into a tight ball as his fists flailed down on me. I didn't want to lose my teeth; they had grown straight like my Dad's. My head seemed to bounce under every hit. I'm not sure how long this went on for but when we arrived home, I ran from the car into one of the outhouses, which had a staff toilet and sink in it. Blood ran from my nose and my head throbbed. I screamed loudly. I cried out to God to help me. I then sat on the floor of the outhouse, sobbing in despair.

The next day I found out it was something to do with a telephone message I had taken, which involved someone who owed them money. For some reason they were angry with me. To this day I cannot make any sense of this or give any reason for their behaviour; it was one of those senseless, unreasonable things. Again, I longed for the good life we had with Nan and Dad, but it seemed a million miles away.

A few days later Zoe and I snuck out and ran to another village about two miles away. We were really hungry so we called in at the local church and ate all their communion wafers! We then went on to Zoe's school friend's house and told her mum about the beatings. I showed her my ear, which was by then as black as the sole of my shoe. Her friend's mum didn't drive so she couldn't take us to town but she advised us to ring social services, so we went to the phone box and did just that.

"Can you come into the office?" The woman asked.

"No. There are no buses and we don't have anyone who can bring us," I replied.

"You need to come in to the office to see us," she insisted. When we realised that no help was coming, we hurried back home. We heard nothing more from social services.

Mum was in a particularly foul mood one day and she threatened to get Wayne to beat us up that night. Zoe and I decided to run for it. I grabbed my coat and my post office savings book but couldn't find my shoes anywhere so I put on some flip-flops, which made it difficult to run through the village. We decided to go across the countryside to a derelict bridge we knew of from our walks. This would take us over the river into another county.

As we hurried across the broken bridge, I struggled to keep my flipflops on. Rubble fell through the gaps with every step and plopped into the river. We eventually got to the other side and found the main road. We both put our thumbs out to passing traffic but no one stopped. We decided to walk to Dad's aunt's house, whilst still trying to thumb a lift. Eventually a vehicle did slow down next to us. It was a police car.

We told the policeman about the beatings and the threats. The officer seemed cross with us. He took us to the station, where another, much nicer officer took over and we repeated our plight. I still did not dare mention the other unspeakable matter though. He took us back to our mum and stepfather.

As we heard their muffled voices downstairs Zoe and I pushed our wardrobe up to our bedroom door. Not that that would stop either of them. We had done this in the past, only to see it fall in with Mum clambering over it in a rage. This time it didn't move and neither did we. I wished we had made it back to Dad and Nan; I longed for the simple, innocent times we spent with them.

Our attempt to run away was not mentioned except that Gary boasted how he had followed us and let Mum know where we were, hence the quick police response. We never heard from the police again.

There was no Childline in those days, there were no mobile phones, only phone boxes and the hotel phone (which we had restricted use of). The internet did not exist then either. We dare not speak to teachers as we felt so ashamed and there were no safeguarding-type systems in place then.

One summer we earned ourselves a ban from leaving the garden. We were not allowed out of the gate during the whole of the six weeks school holidays.

Life went on in a barely tolerable way. I had learned the art of hiding the bad stuff and putting on a good face. Wayne continued to grope and grab me at every opportunity he got, which made me feel sick and sad. I craved normality and wanted my family to appear normal. I willed them to be normal.

References

2.1 Shakespeare W, English Playwright *and Poet (1564-1616). From Sonnet 18.*

2.2 Green P, Blue Horizon, 1979, Albatross instrumental sung by Fleetwood Mac

2.3 Osmonds A, M & W, 1972, MGM Records, Crazy Horses by the Osmonds.

2.4 Diamond N, 1970, UNI Records, Cracklin Rosie sung by Neil Diamond.

"When I am afraid, I put my trust in thee. In God, whose word I praise, in God I trust without a fear. What can flesh do to me?"

Psalm 56 verses 3-4 (RSV)

My Story – Teens - Chapter 3

Renewing my mind

When I was moved into a room with Alison back in the hotel, I was so relieved. I could protect both her and me, as Wayne wouldn't want to wake the baby. We slept together in a single bed, whilst Trish and Zoe had the bunk room.

I wrote in my diary about how much I hated Wayne. I hid this diary in my drawer. He searched through my things when I was at school one day and I was in big trouble when I got home. I didn't get my diary back and after that I only wrote arrangements in diaries, not feelings.

I had been given a Bible at secondary school, which I began to read in my early teens, in the hope that God would help me. Each night I read a few pages with my baby sister asleep beside me. I started at the beginning and ploughed through a lot of dull, difficult bits on to encouraging bits. It was through reading this that I felt better able to cope and my growing faith in God gave me the strength to fight Wayne. I was given hope in reading passages such as:

"Trust in the LORD with all your heart, and do not rely on your own insight."
Proverbs 3 verse 5 (RSV)

"Surely there is a future, and your hope will not be cut off." Proverbs 23 verse 18 (RSV)

I was re-configuring everything in my mind, to look at it from the perspective of the Bible. Readings such as Romans 12 verse 2 (RSV) helped me:

"Do not be conformed to this world but be transformed by the renewal of your mind, that you may prove what is the will of God, what is good and acceptable and perfect." These and many more scriptures helped me to take a stand against my stepfather. I clung to God's promises for my life and every night I prayed God would make me a better person, not better than those around me but a better person than I might be, under the circumstances.

Grandad and Grandma eventually put their differences with Wayne aside and sometimes came to see us and his brother visited too, with his children and grandchildren. One-by-one at least eight people, of all sizes, would clamber out of our great-uncle's big black car, like something out of a comedy sketch.

Cousin Richard was about my age and we became good friends. He spent two of the school summer holidays with us. He was my chaperone who protected me from Wayne for those two summers, without realising he was doing so.

Richard and I got up at six-o'clock every morning to do the manual work needed for the businesses, then we all went out on bikes to the next village for ice lollies. We took it in turns to pedal as we often gave each other a croggy (two-on-a-bike). I felt very sad at the end of both of these summers as we waved Richard off and I was left behind without his friendship and protection.

'Bohemian Rhapsody' by Queen was the theme tune for my memories of the heat wave in 1976.

We all helped at the Queen's Silver Jubilee village party in 1977. I sported a 'Purdy' haircut; very short with a full fringe like Joanna Lumley's character and I wore a trendy striped jumper and blue jeans as I led the pony rides.

I had moments of being angry with God for putting me in, what I sometimes felt was, the wrong family. We children did fall out with each other sometimes. At other times I loved being part of a big family and I enjoyed the feeling of togetherness with my siblings. I felt protective of them all. We were presented as a well-dressed and capable family at the local village pub. We even took part in a talent competition.

"How could such a pretty face make such an awful noise," was some feedback I heard about my singing! In my defence I did have a terrible cold at the time. Woe betide anyone who took an interest in Zoe or me though. One such young man, who could clearly see things weren't as they should be, took it upon himself to follow our children-packed car from the pub on his motorbike. Wayne sped off, then slammed his brakes on, deliberately causing the young man to fall off his bike. He then got out of the car and threatened him before leaving him in the middle of the road.

Breaking the spirit seemed to be Wayne's tactic towards everyone and everything. At one time we had fifteen cats. One of our cats was such a grumpy cat, but when she went to scratch Wayne, he flung her across the room and she hit the wall with a thud. The poor thing was broken and kept out of everyone's way after that. I was determined he wouldn't break my spirit; I had God on my side.

Wayne regularly boasted about how he beat the patients up at the hospital. He said he knew to thump them in their hairline so that the bruising didn't show. He brought medicines and vitamin pills home for us.

Mum and Wayne tried to turn us against Nan and Dad and as children we did begin to feel a bit embarrassed about them. He regularly said with authority that our dad was a psychopath and that Nan was a prostitute (he used the 'w' word). I didn't really know what he meant but I knew it wasn't good and I didn't believe Nan or Dad were bad people. Mum instilled in me the need to protect their family unit; I felt hugely responsible for my siblings.

Wayne repeatedly told me how he could have Zoe committed to an asylum as he said she was like our dad. She had rebelled a bit and got in to smoking and fighting, giving him some ammunition to throw at this argument, so I believed him. I knew I must stay strong, to defend us both in case he ever tried to do this.

Wayne also said that if I spoke up the family would be split up and we would all be put into different council run homes for children. I believed this too and desperately wanted us all to be together.

Wayne regularly told Zoe and me that he knew how to kill a person without leaving any evidence (something to do with air in the blood stream). His mantra of how he could and would murder us and all the family if we spoke up, cut deeply, and we *really* believed he could do this.

Mum was either busy with the businesses or going out to the pub; her attention to all her children was minimal. Zoe and I stepped in to bake cakes, wash our siblings' hair and take them on long walks by the river. Mum resented this and complained to Wayne, who then told me off, shouting:

"You are not the mother!"

"Well tell her to do it then!" I retaliated.

A few times Mum took me shopping with her. I enjoyed these trips and we chatted a bit then. She said I was the one who could sing (questionable) and that I made her laugh. She called me her English Rose.

At other times we clashed head on. She was in such an awful rage one evening, clattering around the kitchen shouting all sorts of threats, that I set off to run away on my own. It was pitch black in the open countryside with no street lights at all but I was so upset I decided to try to get to a larger village four miles away, where a school friend lived with her lovely mum. I made it to the next hamlet about two miles away, but I had forgotten about "rats' hill" (a place on a country lane where farmers dumped manure and where rats swarmed). I could not bring myself to walk by these rats in the pitch black, so I went back to the hamlet and knocked on the door of a bungalow there. A lovely old couple invited me in and phoned home for me. Wayne collected me and took me home, making a joke of it all.

Occasionally we persuaded them to let us go out and at one point they did let us go to the town's teen disco, although he often followed us. The little bit of freedom we had was always interrupted by him driving around the corner or turning up at an event. As his huge profile filled the doorways my heart sank.

I had made some friends at school and was eventually allowed to go to my friend Sally's from time-to-time. Her dad was a successful businessman in the town and Wayne liked to tell people that I was friends with his daughter. They lived in a beautiful big house with carpets that felt as thick as cushions and ensuite bathrooms (unheard of in those days!) I really enjoyed using the ensuite with its avocado suite and brass taps; such luxury after sharing a bathroom with a big family and hotel guests.

It was always Wayne who came to pick me up though, and the twelve-mile journey always included a stop where he attempted to molest me and tried to persuade me to co-operate. I learned the art of distraction to try to get out of these situations with the least contact possible. I talked to him about his daughters and asked him to promise he would not abuse them in this way (I worded this with care). His stock reply was:

"I would never cr*p on my own doorstep."

I pleaded with him not to hurt his children and tried to protect them by distracting him when I could see he was building up to violence, such as when he started to unbuckle his belt, ready to hit them with it.

Wayne consistently tried to persuade me to go along with his abuse. Telling me it was part of nature and hormones and many other long lessons on this theme, including sharing 'secrets' of an adult nature. He offered treats, flirted with me and flattered me. Then, when I did not comply, he insulted me and threatened punishment.

He also had an ongoing theme about being judged by people. He said we should not mention his work at the hospital but put on any school forms that our parents were business executives as we would be better regarded.

I think I parked the abuse somewhere in my brain in my attempt to make it go away, or stop, or not be true. This way I could be a different person at school and with friends. I suffered terrible nightmares though, where I was either falling through a bridge or being crushed by someone.

My school friend, Sally, came to stay with us a couple of times but I made sure she was never alone with Wayne. I remember her looking around in a daze at our old home bulging with people. She seemed entranced by the humour and affection on show, but bewildered by the environment.

On one rare occasion Wayne gave Zoe and me permission to go to an 18th birthday party at a pub. As we settled in with our glasses of lemonade, an older girl, who had worked on our small-holding a few summers before, approached us. As we chatted, she told us how special she was to Wayne, how she still saw him and had been doing for the last few years. She calmly went on to say she had sex with him and had been doing since she was twelve. I started to shake.

It seemed he had persuaded her this was all part of their secret life. She said he had a garage in the town and that he took her there for sex. She told us he gave her lots of treats but also threatened he would kill her if she told her parents. She seemed scared, yet accepting of it all. I pleaded with her not to meet him again.

We hadn't been at the party long before the police raided it. Someone had rung to report underage guests there and the party was shut down. Somehow everyone knew it was our stepfather who had done this and as we walked along the street outside some of the other guests pointed at us and jeered. We both cried.

Wayne appeared very quickly in his car and took us home, before going on his own night out with Mum.

Zoe and I sat on the floor in the lounge bemoaning our plight, trying to think of ways to get away but we despaired at there being no escape. We renamed our home 'the prison.' I felt helpless and worthless. It was only by reading my Bible that I was able to regain hope in such readings as Romans 15 verse 13 (RSV):

"May the God of all hope fill you with all joy and peace as you trust in him, so that you may overflow with hope by the power of the Holy Spirit."

Several times when Wayne was late getting home from work, I wanted to tell Mum I knew where he was (at the garage she didn't even know he had), but I didn't want to upset her and I also wondered if she would believe me; I feared that she would be angry with me for telling her. Wayne found out that I knew about his garage and he took this as an opportunity to get me on board. The next time he picked me up from my friend's house he drove me to a row of garages in the town and asked me to go in with him. I refused. He went on to tell me he had had a vasectomy and explained what this was, so I 'didn't need to worry about anything'. I felt sick and folded my arms tightly as I shook my head. I felt my heart racing under my jumper. He eventually drove off, furiously.

He made his fury clear in subtle ways like staring at me whilst he dished out the dinner, piling the others' plates high and putting a small amount of food on mine. I sat in silence at the table as he took anything I said as an opportunity to punish me. He then shouted at me:

"Don't give me that silent insolence!" I was in trouble again.

Zoe made friends with a lady called Clara who managed a shop in the town and I was eventually allowed to take a Saturday job there. I loved this.

Clara was such a kind, fun-loving person who invited us to her flat after work. This was at the back of a family home and was gated so that even if Wayne followed us there, he would have to get over the bolted gate and through the family's home to get in. He hated Clara for the refuge she gave us.

Clara shared her very fashionable clothes with us. I felt so grown up on a school ice-skating trip wearing her black flares and long khaki grandad shirt. All those skating trips when I was younger paid off and I had a moment in the limelight that evening!

I had boyfriends on-and-off and I sometimes met them in town. When Mum found out about one of them, she called me a prostitute. She gave no guidance on what girls should or should not be doing with boys, but I certainly wasn't doing that! I had some nice boyfriends and some inappropriate ones but kept most of them away from our parents. Bizarrely at one time they let me go out with an older boy who was the son of a local business man, who Wayne seemed to want to impress.

Their parenting was unpredictable, ranging from abandonment to extreme restriction and this left me very confused. I yearned for Nan and Dad and the settled, if unconventional, life we had had with them. The pain of the loss of this was buried, but soothed a little by the good times we had with our siblings.

Wayne threatened us against going out with boys generally but boys with motorbikes were definitely not allowed. He was an out-and-out racist and banned us from going out with any vaguely black boys (he regularly used the 'n' word), on pain of death.

The relationship with Grandad and Grandma was soon under the shadow of Grandma's cancer and they came to live with us at the end. Wayne taunted her about her speech and laughed at her. Grandma made it clear how she felt about Wayne by angrily throwing extra swear words out around him.

Although we had the occasional day trips out, we went away on our only proper family holiday that winter, to a cottage in the middle of nowhere. Wayne's behaviour on this holiday was despicable and Zoe and I were very low at the end of it. Whilst we were away Grandma died in our home. We were all very sad.

The nightmares continued; I often woke up in a state of panic, with my heart racing and my body shaking as I reached for my Bible and found comfort in readings such as Psalm 62 verses 1 -2 (RSV):

"For God alone my soul waits in silence; from him comes my salvation. He only is my rock and my salvation, my fortress; I shall not be greatly moved." Such readings helped restore me to feeling loved and love-able; as I had with Dad and Nan.

The television news continued to report on the strikes in our country and the troubles in Northern Ireland, whilst Abba cheered us on with such songs as 'Dancing Queen'. [Ref 3.1] Snow blizzards cut villages off around this time and once again we were isolated, though there was a mood of everyone pulling together and we were warm and fed. Around the end of the 1970s the first woman prime minister was elected and the winters eventually got a bit better. This made me hopeful that things could change.

My school friend Sally and I were a bit rebellious and used to sneak out at lunchtime to go into town to meet up with boys in the local café. However, we got caught and called to the head teacher's office. But in my last year at secondary school I buckled down and set my heart on a career in journalism while Zoe put her mind to joining the police force. Although she was very bright, she had to leave school at 16 and Mum put her to work in the businesses. Eventually she got a job in a local factory and had very little money; but she had made some new friends. It was when Zoe reached 18 that she broke free. On her birthday, after a violent attack from Wayne she ran from our home and was taken in by a kind lady who worked at the factory. I was so pleased for her that she had escaped, though I was completely bereft, being left behind, without

Zoe. My heart ached every time I came home from school knowing Zoe would not be coming home.

When I was in the build up to my GCSE exams, the family moved house, into the town. Mum and Wayne paid their mortgage off and bought a three-storey hotel from a couple who were volunteers for the Samaritans.

A locked box was put on the inside of the letterbox again, so my post was still vetted but I was allowed one of the rooms on the top floor if I decorated it myself. This was the first time I had had a room of my very own (apart from that night in the mobile home). I used my Saturday job money to buy wallpaper with yellow roses on a white background and I worked out how to put this up. I felt special having my own space to revise for exams and do my schoolwork in.

They continued to take in hotel guests and they applied to be foster parents. They took me along to a training session for this and told me what to say to the fostering assessment team. I was too scared to speak out and part of me hoped things would be okay and that we could be a normal family, able to help others. I willed my family to be normal. Mum was well spoken and articulate and Wayne ran rings around the social worker with his banter. Two foster girls came to live with us. I loved being able to cycle to school now but his constant attentions and Mum's demands for help and money made it difficult to revise. The night before my GCSE maths exam I woke in my new bedroom to find Wayne's huge, clammy body in bed with me. I pushed his big-vested stomach away and quickly jumped out and ran down several flights of stairs to the lounge where hotel guests and some of the family were watching TV.

Wayne always took what he wanted. It haunted me to think he may have been drugging me over the years. I had fought him with everything in me but if he was drugging me (he had brought medicines home from the hospital) it may have been in vain. I buried this thought as I cycled to my exam the next day. I wondered what my Dad was doing; I remembered his gentle singing and his fun ways and I remembered what it felt like to feel safe and special.

Wayne then changed his job to one in which he drove all over the county, so we never knew where or when he would turn up.

For family reasons Clara returned to her home town some miles away and we got a new manager at the shop, where I continued to work on Saturdays. We were sad when Clara left but Wayne was delighted.

Around this time, Wayne was befriended by a local vicar and he took up bell-ringing at his church. I hoped this was an answer to prayer, that my Bible reading was paying off and, that this friendship would help all the family; little did I know what was to come.

More hotel guests meant that Trish and Alison were moved into my room, which was good in one way but meant I now lived in a chaotic, noisy space. Bedrooms were swapped around regularly after that.

When she did get into the police force, in her bid for normality, Zoe treated all the family to a meal in a pub (a rare treat in those days). We had a reasonable evening with all our younger siblings there and we enjoyed hearing about Zoe's new and exciting job. Soon after this

Wayne reverted to form, harassing Zoe, so she kept away again and went to live with Grandad in another town. One day she told Grandad about Wayne's behaviour. Grandad stormed over to our new home and confronted Wayne and Mum about the abuse, in front of all of their children. Mum was devastated but turned to Zoe and told her to: "Go away and die of cancer."

Wayne told Mum we had lured him and that he hadn't been able to resist as we looked so much like her. He spoke a lot more rubbish too. Over and over he repeated his mantras and Mum chose to stay with him. Zoe was banned from seeing any of us, as was Grandad, but we defied this ban by meeting them secretly.

One evening when Wayne was fighting with Mum, David and I stepped in to try to stop it but we couldn't, so I jumped on my bike and pedalled to the house where the people who sold us our new home now lived. As Samaritans I was sure they would help but they just sent me back to see if it had stopped. When I got home, things had calmed down and I heard no more from this couple.

By some miracle I passed my exams and was offered a sixth-form place to study for A-levels. My school friend Sally got a job but another friend, Joanne, stayed on for sixth-form. The work was much harder and those at the top of the classes were extremely bright but I managed to keep up and enjoyed sixth form.

I still felt fearful that someone would find out about my stepfather and that I would be humiliated, so I worked hard, keeping my head down. Joanne and I became good friends and had some nice innocent fun visiting her family, carol singing near Christmas and meeting up. Living in the town made this easier.

When I got home, I was questioned about what I had been doing and then disbelieved. I would be sworn at and accused by Wayne of being a prostitute, amongst other things.

My stepfather's attentions and threats continued and Mum's demands for money from me increased, so at Christmas I had to leave the sixth form to get a job.

I read my Bible and was encouraged by Jeremiah 29 verse 11 (RSV):

"For I know the plans I have for you, says the LORD, plans for welfare and not for evil, to give you a future and a hope."

I secured a full-time job in an office and made some new friends. I became particularly close to a worker there called Josie. I also attended day release and night classes to secure more qualifications.

I started to buy a few little things for myself, including a new blouse to wear the following Saturday. Coming home from work to find twelve-year-old Trish wearing it whilst eating her meal was upsetting and I tried to get her to give it back to me. Wayne walked in to find Trish had me on the floor, proceeded to split us up, and then whacked me across the face. I had reached my limit. I had had enough. I screamed at him. There and then I decided I was prepared to serve a prison sentence if it came to it and in that moment, I really meant what I said:

"You ever touch me again and I will kill you! You will have a knife in your back and you won't see it coming."

I moved out that week into a small flat in the town, at aged 17. Wayne continued to follow, harass and hound me. He peered through the kitchen window counting the cups in the sink (then accused me of having men in the flat), he put cotton across the doorway to check when I was in or out and continued to appear at events I attended. At night I would find it hard to sleep and again reached for my Bible and prayed. Psalm 4 verse 8 (RSV) offered me comfort and I had a sense of God's presence reading:

"In peace I will both lie down and sleep; for thou alone, O Lord, makest me dwell in safety."

I went to friends' parties and I had arranged to have Sally and some friends for a party at my flat one Saturday evening but Wayne's focus was on me that day. He followed me wherever I went and when he caught up with me, he asked me lots of questions. I didn't want friends subjected to this so I cancelled our plans. I eventually lost him and met Sally in a café. I was really fed up. It was then I told Sally about his abuse and about the girl at the 18th birthday party. She was very shocked.

Zoe was hounded by him so much that her bosses issued her with a police radio (there were still no mobile phones) to keep at home. She told her bosses all about Wayne but nothing was done.

Around this time, as I read a newspaper in my lunch-break one day, some extremely distressing news arrived. We hadn't heard from Clara, Zoe's friend and my first manager at the shop, for quite a while. She had been busy and our lives were busy too. But there was her picture in a national newspaper – Clara had been murdered! My heart ached with sadness as I walked around the town sobbing uncontrollably.

Zoe and I were heartbroken but also very unnerved by this incident as we lived under the threat of the same thing happening to us.

References

3.1 Andersson B, Ulvaeu B and Anderson S, 1976, Dancing Queen sung by ABBA

"Do your best and always remember,

the dark clouds pass with time."

Johnnie Ray [Ref 4.1]

My Story – Adulthood - Chapter 4

Reunited

In despair at Wayne's harassment the police transferred Zoe to the city, where we had spent our early childhood. Zoe then set about trying to find Dad and Nan, and with a little help from Nan's old friend she succeeded in tracing their new addresses. She went to see them and arranged for me to meet them a couple of weeks later.

Ten years on, since I last saw him, I walked towards Dad. He was in his car at a T-junction but when he saw me, he jumped out of his car, more or less abandoning it. He ran towards me, grinning from ear-to-ear. He looked older, rounder and more worn down; weathered by life. We hugged and were soon chatting. I can't remember what we talked about only that it was very comfortable and there was a lot of laughter. I felt happy and safe.

We all went to Nan's house. She was much the same as she had always been; aged but ageless. I'd like to say this led to a happy ending but the trials they had both been through, after Zoe and I were snatched from them, had left friction between them. Dad had suffered extreme depression, to the point of being hospitalised. A bottle of sherry every evening seemed to help him cope. He was poor and unwell, yet he battled on as a freelance photo-journalist living on his own in a very small house, where he had a dark room for developing his photographs. This gave the house that same familiar odour of photographic chemicals our early childhood home had. His son was now seven-years-old and lived with his mum.

The week after our reunion Dad wrote to me saying how happy he was to have us back in his life and how much he loved us.

Dad and Zoe came to stay at my little flat one night. Zoe and I slept top-to-tail in my single bed and Dad slept on the two armchairs pushed together. Before we went to sleep, he sang to us: 'The Little White Cloud That Cried'. *Ref 4.1* This was sad but comforting.

Around this time, I met Edward, at a police sports event, where I had gone along to make up the numbers as they were short of women. Zoe introduced us and we ended up playing on the same team. Dad came with us and took photographs of everyone, just as he had done when we were little.

The following week PC Ed called me at my workplace and we started dating.

Mum and Wayne had no idea that we were now seeing Dad and Nan. They did like to tell people I was dating a policeman though and they seemed to accept Ed.

Meanwhile Zoe had started going out with Geoff. Wayne put tacks on Geoff's drive, chased him in his car and harassed his family. Geoff held in there though, and he eventually moved to the city to be with Zoe.

Ed was 19 years-old and had his own car. He helped teach me to drive and we had some fun times, together with Zoe and Geoff. Their families seemed relatively normal.

I told Ed about my stepfather and he was very understanding about it all. We didn't dwell on it and I told him how important it was that we didn't mention it to anyone as my family would be embarrassed and Wayne may murder them and us. He and Geoff respected our position. Romantic and caring, Ed whisked me off my feet, and proposed seven months after we met.

Mum persuaded me to move back home on more favourable terms than my flat so that we could save up the deposit for our new home and save for our wedding.

The wedding preparations got underway, with Wayne's new vicar friend taking a lead. He said it was our marriage but my mother's wedding. It was only when everything was booked and the wedding was getting close that the vicar revealed his true character. The vicar made a pass at Ed; I was devastated. We later found out he had also made a pass at my cousin Richard and were soon aware he had a thing for young men and boys. Trish told me that some of the girls in the church choir had also complained to her about her dad groping them. I was horrified.

When I realised our stepfather's church connections were just as warped as he was, I just wanted to run away to get married. We considered this, but realised it would not be fair to Ed's family.

I was not allowed to have my Dad, Nan or Zoe and Geoff or even Grandad at our wedding. We thought about how we could have our wedding with them and all of Ed's family there and not Mum and Wayne. I knew Wayne would cause deep trouble for everyone, including Ed's family if we did this. I felt I had no choice. I cried for a whole day when I realised that I could do nothing about it. I conformed and my hopes for a normal wedding day slipped away. Mum kept complete control over who could be invited, so friends such as my sixth-form friend Joanne weren't included, though my school friend Sally and my work friend Josie were there.

We were married by a paedophile and I was given away by a paedophile. To everyone else it must have seemed like a lovely wedding, and parts of it were pleasant, including having cousin Richard as an usher, but the day was overshadowed for me.

A month after our wedding, just before Gary's 18th birthday, Wayne beat Trish up really badly. Her fourteen-year-old face and body were covered in bruises. Successfully thumbing a lift, she ran away to Grandad's house. He brought her home and confronted Wayne; again, unsuccessfully.

At Gary's party Wayne was threatening to beat Trish up again. Ed was at work so I was on my own as I pleaded with Mum to protect Trish. I felt desperate to protect her. Mum swore at me, slapped me around the face and sided with him. I took Trish to the phone box nearby, called a taxi and took her to our new home where she stayed for a couple of nights before they demanded she be returned to them.

My husband raised concerns about Wayne's violence towards Trish with his bosses. He was told to drop the subject or risk his job. This was the early 1980s; nobody wanted to know. There was no way we felt able to raise other concerns. We heard no more from the police on this, although Mum and Wayne did stop fostering at around that time.

I decided I did not want to see Wayne ever again and I made this clear to Mum. This hurt me as it would restrict how often I could see my siblings but it was the right thing to do. Wayne's behaviour was evil and I prayed:

"Rescue me, Lord, from evildoers; protect me from the violent, who devise evil plans in their hearts and stir up war every day." Psalm 140 verse 1 (NIV). Mum stood with Wayne again and kept her distance from me.

Wayne still followed me and we wanted to move away, but I needed to complete my qualifications.

After two years in the force Zoe had to leave the police due to the trouble Wayne caused her.

After Gary's 18th birthday I didn't see my mum for well over a year, then around that time, we found out that Wayne had a new distraction: he had taken on a mistress. When Wayne left Mum for his mistress Mum was devastated but it was a happy day for us.

Mum then got in touch with Zoe and me, and we arranged to meet up. As Mum was decrying Wayne, we were allowed, just this one time, to speak a bit about his abuse of us. We talked about Wayne's own daughters, Trish and Alison, and whether they were at risk. We recounted how, when we had voiced our concern for them, he had always crudely said he would never cr*p on his own doorstep.

I made a conscious decision to treat Mum as if she had been a good mum to me and I did this with a good heart. My faith helped me with this. I still read my Bible regularly and prayed for my family. I was strengthened by such verses as 2 Thessalonians 2 verses 16-17 (abridged, NIV):

"May our Lord Jesus Christ himself and God our Father… encourage your hearts and strengthen you in every good work and deed."

There was a part of me that still hoped for normality. Letting go of resentment towards my mum, about how she had treated us, in exchange for the possibility of a good relationship with her seemed a good choice and we mostly got on well.

Dad and Nan joined us for some social occasions and there was a sort of truce, even peace between them and Mum and Grandad. We had some nice times together.

Meanwhile, Wayne was busy with his new lady and seemed oblivious to us for a while, so Zoe was able to get married to Geoff with all the family there. With a baby on the way their winter wedding was a happy day. Dad gave Zoe away with Nan, all our siblings, aunties, cousins and Mum and Grandad there, all dressed in their finery.

I sobbed with happiness for Zoe. I cried through the whole service; it was so beautiful. Not the most attractive look for the chief bridesmaid though! I think there was an element of sadness in my tears too, as I had not been able to have them all at our wedding.

Mum came to the wedding with her new boyfriend, who was a nice man with two young children. When Wayne found out about him, he went to Mum's new house and trashed the vehicle in her drive, making in un driveable. Fearful for his children, her boyfriend ended the relationship.

After the wedding we heard that Wayne's mistress had ended their relationship. Soon after this her house burnt down.

Wayne caused everyone so much trouble (including his mistress's new boyfriend) and I feared for our safety, so although I knew I would miss my younger siblings, we decided to move away. I had passed my exams and achieved promotion in my office career, then gave this up and moved away.

Like any young couple we relished embarking on our new life together. There was the added hope that establishing our own home and family life elsewhere would help to put the past traumas behind me. Perhaps we could feel safe and free from the hurt and fear, but it was not going to be as easy as that. I felt as though I had survived a ten-year accident and emerged running from the scene, trying not to look back, not wanting it to be true. The lack of response from social services, the police and even the Samaritans and our experiences of the vicar left me feeling powerless. I feared Wayne but tried to put him out of my mind. We found a lovely old house in a village nearer to the city. The day we moved in we found out I was expecting our first baby and we were elated. Our new life was starting and hopes for normality returned. I remembered what Jesus said in John 10 verse 10 (RSV):

"The thief comes only to steal and kill and destroy; I came that they may have life, and have it abundantly."

'Sunshine days' is how Zoe describes that summer when her baby was born.

The following February with thick snow on the ground, our own baby Rebecca arrived. The house was freezing but we were very happy. I was in awe of the responsibility of a new baby and extremely mindful of her being treated well. She didn't sleep much and we were both exhausted. Although a perfect daddy by day, my husband did not cope well with broken nights. With some support from Nan and Ed's family we struggled through. We had Rebecca christened at the local church with Sally, Geoff and Zoe as Godparents.

Dad, Nan, Mum, Grandad and all our siblings were invited to every celebration. Dad started to decline invitations more and more though and seemed increasingly uncomfortable with our mum.

We were happy when we found out we had another baby on its way, but this was short-lived, as I had a complicated miscarriage, which made us doubt that we could have any more children and left my health under threat. We were both hurting and our marriage was under strain.

I went back to work part time in an estate agent's office and we somehow came to terms with our loss. Ed and I weren't getting on well though and I started to look at some of the small houses coming on to the market, with a view to moving out with Rebecca.

I was also looking at the people going in and out of the church near our house and one Sunday, whilst Ed was at his Sunday morning football game I decided to go and give it a try.

With Rebecca at my side I was welcomed by the people there. Many of them chatted to us at the end and they told me about the Sunday school they ran in the other room. I enjoyed the warmth of the people and the uplifting songs we sang.

I started to attend more regularly but I went into the Sunday school with Rebecca. I was unable to trust even the nicest of people after my experiences with Wayne and the vicar.

One night I dreamed that Rebecca was walking away with her daddy, as if she was going on an access visit. When I woke up in tears, I decided that one of us had to save our marriage. Even though I wasn't feeling particularly loving towards him, I decided to start doing nice things for Ed and booked some surprise events. The most memorable was when I booked a holiday abroad for us as a family, which I somehow kept as a surprise for him until we were at the airport!

Our marriage eventually got back on track, and I went to church on Sundays whilst Ed went to play football. He often teased me about 'joining the happy-clappy brigade,' but he was appreciative of the friendship the people at the church gave us, and of how welcome they made him at social events.

I struggled when preachers talked about us needing to forgive those who had hurt us, which is a message given most weeks in church and is encouraged in the Lord's prayer in Matthew 6 verse 12 (NIV):

"And forgive us our debts as we also have forgiven our debtors" I wanted to forgive but felt like shouting:

"HOW?!"

I still read my Bible every night but when I heard Ed coming up the stairs, I stopped reading and hid it.

I kept Christian teaching notes from various seminars I went to and soaked up as much learning about God as I could. The more I learnt, the more I heard from God in my prayers.

Meanwhile Trish had two lovely children and Zoe had her second, beautiful baby. Eventually we were expecting our second baby. As our baby grew my faith also strengthened, and when I was heavily pregnant, I was confirmed at our local church, choosing the song: 'One More Step Along the Way I Go,' *Ref 4.2* for this service. A friend was confirmed at the same time and chose 'All Things Bright and Beautiful.' *Ref 4.3*

When Rebecca was four, after a precarious pregnancy, Amy was born. 'Babies don't always come easily' is what we learned and we treasured our two girls. What a lovely surprise then, when just over a year later, after an equally troublesome pregnancy, our wonderful son Lewis was born. We were exhausted but happy and our family was complete.

I had many internal conversations with myself; I was determined not to become an over-protective parent and that our children would have the right amount of freedom to live healthy, balanced lives. I was also very aware of potential risks and alert to keeping them safe. With zero inclination to behave in an abusive way and with such an appreciation of the damage abuse does I knew I would guard any child with my life. I also knew that whilst my Dad was not perfect, he was loving and kind to me; this helped me to accept God as my ultimate loving father and I aspired to honour him in the way I parented our children.

When Trish got married Wayne gave her away. Having just had our son I felt vulnerable but I decided to just go to the service, for Trish, with my husband as support. I sat at the back of the registry office but could see that same broad, pink, pimply neck. My heart beat quickened as flashbacks to my childhood rushed into my mind. I held my baby close and we left after the service. Zoe was pregnant with her third child and understandably stayed away.

Our own family life was full and relatively normal. We had Amy and Lewis christened at the local church. By this time Dad did not attend if Mum was going to be there, so we had separate celebrations with him.

Dad was always lively and innovative. He was the first person I knew of to have a mobile phone. He was the first to embrace new ideas and new people of all nationalities and he encouraged us to do the same. He was also starting to show some signs of dementia.

I saw Zoe and Trish with their children regularly but I was quite isolated day-to-day and often felt alone, even lonely as a mum of three under-fives. In my prayers I felt God say I was *'set apart for a good reason.'*

I continued to go to church each week with our three children, eventually entrusting them to the lovely Sunday school teachers there, whilst I received the gentle teaching in the main service. I sat at the back of the church as the stories I had read in my Bible were brought to life in song and in the teaching. I heard of the suffering Jesus endured and of his death and resurrection; of how he gave us the Holy Spirit to guide us in this life and lead us in to the next; I felt his overwhelming love and compassion and sensed his presence with me. Sometimes hot tears fell down my cheeks. We became part of a lovely church family.

One of the older ladies kindly opened her house to mums and babies every Wednesday afternoon, which was some compensation for having no family living locally. When one of the mums told the group that her neighbour had abused her when she was four and it continued for years, I was stunned. I said some comforting things, but one lady told her: "You just have to forgive him." I wanted to scream. I had no idea what to do or what to say.

Soon after I visited a lady from another church as I desperately needed to talk to someone about my experience, but not someone I saw every week. As I sat in her front room, I could not speak so she suggested I write a few things down about the unspeakable matter. She read these and prayed over them. She also suggested that I distanced myself from my mum more.

Meanwhile, following her divorce from Wayne, Mum had moved in with a new man whose own children were more grown up. He tolerated her big family and we had some reasonable times when we got together. Mum was never maternal or of much help, but she did like to have everyone together from time-to-time.

On the extremely rare occasions Mum looked after our children I was insistent that Wayne was not allowed anywhere near them. Mum dismissed this concern saying:

"You don't need to worry about him, he's just an old man,"

"God doesn't pay his debts in money," and

"Vengeance is mine says the Lord." As a non-church goer she was not afraid to try to speak for God. When we did try to talk about the past, she silenced us, saying:

"Look how well you've done. What happened to you made you stronger."

"We did well despite what happened to us, not because of it," was my reply, and I really felt this was true. I fought against the feelings of shame and of being tainted and probably over-compensated in my efforts as a parent, by expecting high standards of myself in protecting and caring for our children.

I also struggled with my mum saying horrible things about my real dad, whilst we were not allowed to speak about our stepfather's abuse over the years. Many times, I drove the 20-miles journey home from visiting her, quietly shedding tears. After one of these times, when she was about ten-years-old, Rebecca took it upon herself to find our writing paper and stamps. Without us knowing she posted a letter to her Nan telling her off for being horrible to me. After some resistance Mum did, partly, take this on board. When she reverted to form, six-year-old Amy challenged her to her face; they had a bit of a love-hate relationship! I discouraged them in this but they seemed to have their own sense of righteous anger.

Whilst 'putting a good face on' I struggled with associations triggering unwelcome memories, which often led to a sort of re-living of the feelings around these. Wayne had a strong regional accent, which made me wary of men with this accent and I had to keep re-programming my thinking. If I heard someone expressing hateful or bigoted opinions or swearing near me, I could stay calm at the time, but I felt my anxiety levels rise massively and I would shake afterwards.

I was accused a couple of times of being over-sensitive on child protection issues relating to the potential for violence or harm, 'due to having been abused'. In both cases, sadly, my instincts were later proven to be correct. In one case the person attacked someone and was arrested and in the other the person had to be reported to the police for very serious stalking. I felt I was just more aware, not over-sensitive.

Over the years I pleaded with our siblings to make sure Wayne was not near any children in his new relationships. Wayne had several relationships and lived at many different addresses over the years and he usually had at least two vehicles. Ed always let the local police know where Wayne lived, and told them about his risk to children. The police were a bit more receptive then and called this 'intelligence sharing.'

Zoe and I sometimes discussed reporting Wayne to the police properly but we feared his oft-repeated threats would be carried out on us or our children. We feared he would mow them down in his car or abduct them. We also had Mum constantly drilling it into us that we would bring shame on the family if we reported Wayne and that it would make her ill. So, with no support available and with the threats over us, we dismissed this as an option.

I strived so hard and felt driven to succeed. I felt as if I could run my charger at anything life threw at me. I vowed to myself not to be like my mum. When the children were little I volunteered at various groups. I helped facilitate parenting classes and ended up getting more out of these than those I was helping! A course on being assertive was a revelation to me. Amongst other things this course taught me that I had the right to be treated with respect and a responsibility to treat others with respect and to stand up for those whose rights were not being respected. I had only ever thought of my responsibilities; no one ever told me I had any rights. I read the book cover-to-cover on the first day I received it. I was determined to cut my own path as a parent and these courses helped my confidence with this.

During this time, I also ran my own, successful business.

Our sister Alison was a fun aunty who was very involved with all the nieces and nephews. When she was older, she lived with Zoe in the city for a year whilst she went to college there. She then moved away to pursue her career, though she did come home regularly.

We siblings were very close as adults and we supported each other, never using 'half-brother' or 'half-sister' as a description of our relationship. Birthdays and Christmases were party times and we met up as regularly as we could in between, with all our children, who loved being together.

At family weddings and parties, we all danced together to such songs as 'We are Family.' *Ref 4.4* I was the least 'cool' of them all in that I could never remember bands' names or song titles. But I referred to our relationship as brothers and sisters as 'the force' as I felt the bond between us was so strong. They seemed to appreciate that we were carrying the burden of Wayne's crimes.

I struggled when our siblings talked about Wayne as if he was a normal dad though. They described him as having 'alpha-male' behaviour and gave Wayne the nick-name 'Wild-Wayne,' which they used fondly. This seemed to mock his actions, whilst trying to make them acceptable somehow. This was like using billows to fan the flame of my low, smouldering indignation and I discreetly left the room when this happened.

References

4.1 Johnnie, Ray 1951; from The Little White Cloud That Cried song.

4.2 Carter, Sydney Bertram, 1971, Stainer & Bell Ltd, One More Step Along the Way I Go song.

4.3 Alexander, Cecil F, 1848, All Things Bright and Beautiful song.

4.4 Edwards B and Rodgers N,1979, Atlantic Records We are Family sung by Sister Sledge

"We have looked the beast in the eye.

Our past will no longer keep us

hostage."

Archbishop Desmond Tutu [Ref 5.1]

My story – Adulthood - Chapter 5

Facing the Beast

I visited Grandad every week towards the end of his life and we had a very comfortable relationship. His funeral marked a sad time for all the family.

Nan had become Nan to all our siblings and they all loved her, everybody did. Her death was another terrible blow for us all. The day she died Zoe took me a walk around all the parks we had played in when we lived with Nan and Dad as children. I hadn't been back to these since we were snatched away. We walked by our early childhood home and wandered by our lovely primary school. Happy memories flooded back. I wondered why we had had this taken from us. I cried the whole time.

After Nan's death Dad gradually became more unwell so we moved him to supervised living accommodation and as his dementia developed, we eventually moved him to a residential home.

We had lots of friends and some very close ones; some we took regular holidays with. I kept in touch with my friend Josie from the office. Josie became a Christian at her local church and was a wonderfully honest and forthright friend. We met up regularly with our families. I talked to her about most things but I didn't tell her about the abuse. Church was still new to me but Josie spoke openly about her faith and often prayed out loud for me. She prayed over my dad as he was deteriorating physically and mentally.

Josie explained that we are in a spiritual battle and led me to 2 Corinthians 10:4 (NIV):

"The weapons we fight with are not the weapons of the world. On the contrary, they have divine power to demolish strongholds."

I was re-assured when Dad came to church with me and affirmed his faith in God. I took him out once a week, with our children. He was very gentle and fun with them, but he became more like another child to me, which I found hard. Dad did manage to come to my 40th birthday party, despite our mum being there. His dementia was clearly increasing as demonstrated when he skipped the main course and ate five portions of pavlova! It was rather nice pavlova made by a friend from church. Dad took to the dance floor with me at this party and I treasure that moment.

Josie, my school friend Sally and another close friend, Marie, sang on the karaoke with me at this party. Josie had a head scarf on as she was being treated for cancer.

I was devastated when she died a few months later, in her early forties. I think about her regularly and I read the Christian daily reading book she gave me every day.

Soon after Josie's funeral Sally got married. We drank far too much champagne and danced all night, which shelved some of the blues, for that night at least.

Gynae surgery was next on my agenda. It took some time for me to recover from the operation, but I went back to work as soon as I could. The flashbacks and the night terrors increased.

Ed had started coming to church with me and after some time he became a Christian. It felt as if our marriage had grown into a three-dimensional one and we enjoyed our shared faith.

Around this time, I found out that my cousin Richard had also become a Christian. His lovely wife had led him to faith. He and I were the only ones in our wider family who were practicing Christians. He had moved away and had a very successful career and a busy family life so we only caught up at weddings and funerals, but I took heart from the fact that the bond we built over those two summers now extended to our shared faith. When we found out that he too had cancer we made more effort to get together as families. His death was a massive loss for us all, not least his wife and young family.

Sadly, after this Zoe and Geoff split up. This was a very difficult time as it touched on the nerves of us growing up in a broken home and I felt overwhelming sadness.

Zoe had a new man in her life now; a very nice man who supported Zoe in ways she hadn't experienced before. Marcus brought a new dimension to the family but I still felt sad for Geoff and for their children.

Zoe told Marcus everything. He had had a relatively normal upbringing and could not believe how the family had swept Wayne's crimes under the carpet and he was outraged about it.

When Alison got married to Oliver that Christmas, we all took part in the celebration enthusiastically. This was a lovely occasion, made possible by the fact that Wayne was unable to be there.

The following year I had to have a spinal operation and this left me weakened. Despite this I did go back to work but exhaustion seemed to haunt me. Flashbacks to my childhood invaded my thoughts with minimal prompting and this left me feeling quite down at times.

One evening, as I travelled home on the train, after attending a prestigious award ceremony at which a company I represented was recognised, I burst into tears. I should have been feeling elated by the success of this trip but I could not stop the tears from falling. This and other similar incidences made me see that my 'charger' had burnt out and I had to close my business.

Further surgery left me with still more restrictions on my health. I felt like a bottle about to pop and thought I might just stop the postman and tell him all my woes! So, I paid for a private counsellor as I didn't want the 'shame' of needing counselling to be on my doctor's record. I had developed a sense of shame during the ten years living with an abuser. This was not only in relation to the abuse, but also with regard to how others might judge me in my career, my home and in life generally. I also felt under pressure to be strong so that if Wayne ever tried to use our mental health against us, he would have nothing on me.

The counselling was very helpful. After one session I burnt all but one of our wedding photographs with Wayne on and I felt a bit of release by doing this. I couldn't afford to keep paying though, so I eventually had to park my concerns about shame and my doctor put my name down for six weeks counselling in the surgery, which was also helpful.

My GP also referred me to a psychologist for some longer-term help but there was a huge waiting list, so I self-referred to ISAS (Incest and Sexual Abuse Survivors charity). After a few months a wonderful lady was assigned to me. She spent some time each week helping me to open up about my experience and the tears fell. Sometimes I came out of these sessions feeling lighter, sometimes I felt angry and at other times I felt as if I was dragging my innards along the street. After one session I was so angry I genuinely considered going to confront Wayne at his new home 70 miles away. I bought supplies at the supermarket, fuel for my car and I let Ed know my plans. As I was about to set off, I took a phone call from Zoe; she had a family emergency and needed my help so I abandoned my plans and went to her instead. I'm not sure my resolve would have lasted the 70-mile journey but I never regained that anger-energy enough to consider confronting Wayne directly again. Fear of his threats set in once more, though I was feeling more and more that I should report him to the police.

Eventually my psychologist appointment came through. A psychologist spent an hour a week with me and helped me to understand how my experience had affected me and how I could reclaim some areas of my life. It helped me to come to terms with what had happened to me and affirmed that the people who were supposed to care for me had broken that trust, tried to break me and abused their position of authority.

I realised the abuse had left me with low self-esteem and a lack of self-confidence, and that whilst I had been able to hide behind my achievements and wear a 'brave-face mask' to the world, the harm of the abuse had been eating away at me inside.

I described these counselling sessions as being like spring-cleaning, in that I had to get all the mess out of the corners in order to throw some things away and put the rest back in an orderly way. Amongst other things, my psychologist encouraged me to be less self-critical, to set myself more realistic goals and to use alternative ways to cope.

Around this time, I came across a meditation CD, called 'Inspiring Calm' [Ref 5.11] in which Bible verses are read over relaxing music. I found myself in God's presence each time I listened to this, with a calm coming over me. I listened to it every day.

During the time I was having counselling, and as our children were older, I thought it was time I told them about my past. Trish had moved away but she had told her children all about the abuse, and I didn't want ours to find out from them. Our children all knew my childhood had been difficult but they didn't know the details. It was Amy who asked me directly when she was about eighteen, so I followed her prompt. She cried and was angry. I told Rebecca afterwards. She was angry with Wayne and with her nan but she was understandably worried about the upset, talking about this might cause. Lewis was driving when I told him and his knuckles whitened as he gripped the steering wheel, whilst expressing his anger.

All the counsellors had given Zoe and me the opportunity to report Wayne to the police, but so deep was our fear of his retaliation and so powerful was the grooming by him and our mum, about her health and about the shame we would bring on the family by reporting Wayne, that we had always reluctantly dismissed this as an option. I had felt ready to report him at one time but Zoe was going through her divorce so she was not able to handle reporting at that time and my fear of his reprisals was still very real.

I started to tell some friends about my experience and most were extremely kind and sensitive. One friend cried, another was angry and all of them were supportive. Someone speculated that our abuser may have been abused. There was never any suggestion that he had been abused. Our abuser took what he wanted without regard for his victims. He knew it was wrong as he threatened to kill us if we spoke up. One person said paedophilia was an illness and that they couldn't help themselves. My experience was that Wayne's crimes were not impulsive; he premeditated his attacks on me, he was totally in control and he helped himself to whatever he wanted in his life.

My doctor pointed out to me that as an adult I should feel more able to report him, which was a reasonable person's evaluation; but Wayne was not a reasonable person and he posed a real threat to all of us. Zoe and I would both need to feel in a strong and safe position to go to the police. Ed continued to update the police regularly about Wayne's whereabouts and about the risk of him being around children. This intelligence sharing seemed to be taken more seriously then.

I still pleaded with my siblings to reassure me that Wayne was not around any children, which they did. I was so distressed about this possibility that on one occasion I said to Gary:

"If you didn't know what was happening in the next room how can you be sure he is not doing something to someone now?" Gary told me that he had witnessed Wayne's abuse, most specifically on that one holiday we had been on. He was confident he could keep an eye on Wayne.

Trish spoke to us about Wayne's abuse on several occasions. She was very angry with her dad and said she had witnessed his abuse throughout her childhood and was terrified she would be next. Trish suffered dreadful night-terrors.

Our own dad died in his early seventies, after a drawn out run of bad health. I was sad but also relieved for him. His life had been so hard. He believed in God and I felt sure he was in God's care now. The line in a hymn I knew seemed fitting for his funeral:

"Bright skies will soon be over me, where darkest clouds have been," *Ref* *5.3* All those feelings of loss returned and my sadness for Dad was often consuming, but I held on to Romans 8 verses 38-39, which was read at his funeral and says:

"For I am convinced that neither death nor life, neither angels nor demons, neither the present nor the future, nor any powers, neither height nor depth, nor anything else in all creation, will be able to separate us from the love of God, which is in Christ Jesus our Lord."

A new life was to join the family soon though; Alison was pregnant. When her baby was born, we were delighted. She was the image of

Alison, and therefore she also looked like Wayne, but we loved her even so. We regularly went to see her, taking our mum, our children, or just on our own.

Eventually Alison and her husband Oliver decided to move back to her home town, to be nearer to us all. We were so pleased and we helped them move into their new rural home. However, a difficult conversation was necessary. They would be living just a few miles from her father. Our girls were young ladies and I didn't want them, our son or myself, to even be in the same room as Wayne. She was close to our children and enjoyed their company and their help, and she knew Wayne's history. When I asked Alison if she would visit her dad in his home rather than have him come to hers it was not well received. Her husband, Oliver, was not aware of Wayne's crimes so he was bewildered by this request.

I planned to discuss the abuse with Oliver, now they had a daughter of their own and lived near Wayne. I had a friend whose father had abused her as a teenager. She had planned to protect her daughter when she neared her teens. Sadly, her father started to abuse his granddaughter when she was just four-years-old. This made me realise patterns can change with paedophiles and that any reassurances about Wayne's own children and grandchildren being safe were not to be trusted, so I was planning to speak to Oliver.

When Zoe was due to re-marry, Wayne let it be known that he still held a threat over us. He told Trish that he knew exactly where and when the wedding was in such a way that Trish was worried and alerted Zoe. Such was the dread of Wayne turning up and hurting Zoe or one of the family that they cancelled the wedding. They did marry eventually though and the parties and gatherings continued.

During this time, we felt drawn to follow our children to the new church they were part of in a nearby town. They had all stopped going to our church in their teens and we didn't force the issue. On their own initiative they had eventually all started going to this new church.

Ed and I were both very much attached to the people at our old church. But the storm that was about to hit meant I needed all the support I could get. I can see now why God was drawing us towards this new church… he had put all the right people around us there ready for the next challenging season.

Our children all chose, independently and at different times, to be baptised at their new church. Although they had been christened, this was their adult declaration of their faith. It was on my heart too. I saw it as a new beginning and a sort of washing away of the past. Jesus was baptised and said:

"Therefore, go and make disciples of all nations, baptizing them in the name of the Father and of the Son and of the Holy Spirit and teaching them to obey everything I have commanded you. And surely, I am with you always, to the very end of the age."
I saw from Matthew 28 verses 19-20 (NIV) that it was also a matter of obedience.

Mum, Alison, Oliver and Gary came along to my baptism. I shared some of my story with the congregation, without any details that might distress them, or others. I spoke about believing in a creator God and of Jesus being someone who walked and talked with me every day.

After that I went on the 'Freedom in Christ Ministries' [Ref 5.2] course, which ran for about twelve weeks. This helped me enormously in looking at the truths in life and at what God says about me: my identity. The course instilled into me how valuable I am, and we all are, to God. Something that stood out to me was that in any situation the truth is the truth even though we each see it from our own perspective.

I continued to struggle with preachers in church saying we must forgive. I knew this, and I wanted to, but I didn't know what forgiveness looked or felt like and I still had the urge to stand up and shout out: "HOW?!" This course helped to show me how to forgive and how to be released from the hurt.

Towards the end of the course there was an away-day where we put some of the things we had learnt into practice. The course included 'steps to forgiveness.' [Ref 5.2] These steps encouraged people to forgive others, themselves and God. As part of this, in private, I read a prayer over Wayne. My prayer was:

"Lord, I desire to be free from the hurt and the hate of offences in my past. Today I move beyond desiring to forgive, to asking your help to forgive. Lord, I forgive Wayne for using and abusing me." [Ref 5.2]

It was after praying this prayer over my stepfather, without anyone except Ed knowing about the prayer, that things shifted massively.

The following Saturday Zoe and I were due to go to the pub with our mum, our siblings and their partners. That morning I received a call from Mum to say that our stepfather had been rushed into hospital and that he was probably going to die. Mum had been divorced from Wayne for over 20 years but she was concerned that Zoe and I should be very supportive of our siblings that night.

After the call ended, I sat down and cried. Why was I crying? For them? For us? For him? Because I had prayed the forgiveness prayer over him that very week? Because Mum had yet again put the burden of him on us, whilst all these years insisting on our silence? My reaction was unfathomable. I did not want Zoe to be caught off guard, so once I had calmed down, I rang her to relay Mum's call.

Her reaction was more dramatic than my own. She was just coming to the end of another round of counselling. The week before her counsellor had discussed the option of finally reporting Wayne.

Zoe said she was angry because no one in the family had acknowledged his abuse, and although they all knew about it, we were not allowed to discuss it, and he was going to die having got away with it. In her despair she sent a text message to all the family and to all their partners (who didn't know about the abuse) sharing some of the explicit details. She copied me in. As I read the text message my stomach churned. This stark disclosure of our suffering took my feet from under me. I slumped on the bed, shaking.

Seeing the so-long-silenced details in writing made me feel ill. At the same time, I felt Zoe was right - the suffering Wayne had caused should be acknowledged, before he died and they all slipped into mourning.

I struggled along to the pub with my husband, hoping that the love we had all shared would carry us through this, and there would be mutual support. Zoe felt unable to go. Alison was ill so didn't go.

Silence from Mum again though. Nothing mentioned about the texts, then or the next time I saw her. No words of comfort, no acknowledgement. She left Zoe a 'there, there but keep quiet' type message the following week. Her partner left a nasty message after this, berating Zoe for bringing this up.

Gary phoned Zoe and me. Initially he seemed to be offering support but then went on to cross-question us about the details of the abuse. David said his motto was 'DGI' (don't get involved).

Alison met me twice to try to find a way forward and we discussed the possibility of us reporting Wayne to the police. She said she would always choose Zoe and me, whatever.

Mum sent an email to me accusing us of making her ill, by even discussing the matter. Mum had managed the silence over the years, constantly telling Zoe and me it would make her ill and bring shame on the family if we reported Wayne. She regularly reminded us of his threats to murder us all, and she continued in this vein.

In the car on the way to our mum's 70th birthday party Zoe disclosed the abuse to her grown-up children. They were stunned by this revelation but they smiled for the photographs. It was our ingrained job to keep everyone happy. It seemed our children were falling into the same role.

Wayne did not die but was discharged from hospital and eventually settled in to a care home. Alison asked me for advice about his care and I said I felt he would receive better care in a nursing home.

Wayne was left unable to drive and for the first time in our lives we felt relatively safe, now he was immobile. For the first time in our lives we both felt we had the strength and support to report him to the police; but deciding whether or not to report him was not going to be easy.

References

5.1 Gish, Steven. Desmond Tutu, A Biography 2004. Tutu was Chair of The South African Truth & Reconciliation, Commission, which looked into human rights abuses around apartheid. Tutu is also the author of several books on forgiveness.

5.11 Mansfield, John, Inspiring Calm 2006

5.2 Freedom in Christ course books by Neil T Anderson and Steve Goss (see www.ficm.org.uk) 2017.

5.3 In Heavenly Love Abiding (Waring Ann L. 1850)

"Act justly, love mercy and walk humbly with your God."

Micah 6 verse 8 (abridged from NIV)

My Story – Adulthood -Chapter 6

Confronting the crime

In 2010 media coverage of paedophiles being reported to the police or taken to court was extremely rare (the Jimmy Savile case had not yet been uncovered), so there was very little information on how to go about this. We felt as if we were in un-chartered waters. Before we worked out how it was done, we had to decide whether to report Wayne to the police or not. This was my agony and I prayed endlessly.

David and his girlfriend came for tea one night. We didn't discuss his dad or the text messages directly, but I told them that it was my faith that had got me through this far. I found it hard to talk to my siblings about my faith as it felt like the most personal thing for me, and I suppose for them too.

Gary rang Zoe and me, and he said he thought we would 'probably feel better than we ever had', if we reported the abuse to the police. He seemed to be supporting us but he then grilled us about all the details: "That thing before your maths exam doesn't count because you were sixteen," he announced dismissively (and incorrectly).

I wanted to make it all okay for everyone in the family and to try to help them with their feelings about this, but many times during my prayers I had a very real sensation of someone holding me in the crook of my elbows, from behind and this repeated phrase kept coming to me: *'hands off!'* So, I held back.

"He's just an old man," now rang forth from our siblings. We agreed to have a break from each other for a while, whilst things settled down. One friend gave me a pretty journal notebook and I decided to write things down to try to make sense of everything. I have kept a journal on-and-off since then. I reflected on many Bible verses in this journal such as Psalm 46 verse 1 (NIV):

"God is our refuge and strength, an ever-present help in trouble." These were troubled times and I leaned into Jesus.

I was so worried about how the reporting process would affect our siblings, and this had a huge hold on me until someone asked me how old they all were, and I realised they were all near to middle-age; old enough to handle this. I also found out that, as victims of sexual assault, we had lifelong anonymity and we could ask that Wayne had anonymity too if we felt it would protect our anonymity. On the other hand, publicity would give his other victims a chance to come forward, so this was a decision to consider carefully.

I emailed my siblings to say we needed their support and sent them the link to ISAS for them to get support for themselves.

One of the leaders in our new church was a retired professor of criminal law. I arranged to meet him and told him about the abuse and spoke to him of my dilemma.

"You've been through hell!" He said, then calmly reflected the options I had mentioned back to me and offered support and wisdom. Then he prayed. I could then see that in the past we didn't speak out due to fear of Wayne's reprisals and fear of shame and that to not act now would be another fear-based choice.

Another friend of ours was the police chief superintendent for our area, who had been on the same Christian camping holidays as us. Ed spoke to him and he offered his support too.

I sought advice from close friends who were Christians, and close friends who were not. I fell on my knees in prayer at church and at home to plead with God to guide me. I called the NAPAC helpline [Ref 6.0] for advice and the UCB prayer-line [Ref 6.1] to ask for prayer. The support from these and from previous counselling helped me to understand that in reporting Wayne we would be handing him back his property (his shame) and hopefully giving release to other victims. I prayed and read my Bible and felt that, when we had done our part, God would do his:

"For the battle is not yours but God's." 2 Chronicles 20 verse 15 (NIV)

I thought about the next generation, of how our action in finally reporting could help protect them by challenging the formula used by perpetrators. The Manic Street Preacher's lyrics played over in my mind: "If you tolerate this, then your children will be next." [Ref 7.1]

Reporting Wayne was not about taking revenge (which was impossible anyway) but about seeking release from the lies that had held the family for 40 years. It was about seeking truth and release for Zoe, for me and for other victims. I did not want to hurt Wayne but I did want him to be held **accountable** and for his crimes to be **acknowledged.** I wanted him to have a chance to be sorry; to **apologise.**

A team from our church ran regular services in the local sex offenders' prison and they reported that the care there was good, so I knew he would be well looked after if he went to prison.

Ed attended a conference with Retired Chief Constable Robin Oake (see quote in Chapter 8 [Ref 8.1]) whose son Stephen was murdered a few years before, whilst on duty in the police. Ed spoke to him of our dilemma and he said we were doing absolutely the right thing in seeking justice. They prayed over this.

The question that I asked myself, which finally swayed me was:

"If I, as a middle-aged woman, with all this support, felt unable to report, how would a child ever feel able to report this crime?"

In my Our Daily Bread [Ref 6.2] reading Marvin Williams spoke about justice needing to be done, but in the hands of God or the authorities ordained by God. UK laws were founded on Christian principles so we resolved to report Wayne's crimes to these authorities: the police.

I kept checking my motives. There was no way we could avenge or punish our perpetrator that would equate to the crimes he had committed against us, nor did we want to but we did desire some fairness. Mercy and compassion were at the front of my thoughts but righteousness and justice needed to be sought. For me speaking out drew a line in the sand, cut through the babble of minimisation and justification and released Zoe and me and all of the family from the burden of fear and shame.

We rang the police and were booked in to the police's specialist unit, which had only been set up for a couple of years. We arrived at what looked like an ordinary house and were welcomed by the support staff. They explained the reporting process to us. They listened to us and answered our questions, but they did not put us under any pressure to report. They gave us a few leaflets and the 'From Report to Court' [Ref 6.3] handbook, which laid out the facts around the crimes, including the possible outcomes. This informed me that what Wayne had done to me (I have spared the reader the explicit details) could, under current legislation, lead to life imprisonment. He was old so even if he was convicted, I realised he would not serve much of a sentence. I also recognised that no sentence, however long, would give us our childhood back. Reading this handbook and the cold facts in it increased my confidence in reporting our perpetrator.

We made our decision to report and we were re-booked in to their centre to give statements to the police the following week. Zoe and I decided not to speak to each other at all about what we would tell the police so that our words would be our own.

Zoe was interviewed first. For a while I sat in a small room upstairs in the house with the TV on and magazines to read, but I couldn't concentrate so I went out for a walk around the housing estate and over the open green parkland.

"Where are you God?" I cried out quietly. "Where are you? I need you here now!" I was reminded in my prayers of what God assures us of many times in the Bible (here from Joshua 1:5 NIV):

"I will never leave you nor forsake you."

Several hours later Zoe reappeared, looking pale and washed out, but relieved. After their cigarette break the two policewomen led me into a small room downstairs. I sat on the two-seater sofa facing a camera. One officer interviewed me from an arm chair, whilst the other looked in from the adjoining room, recording us via a video camera. We were told that Wayne would see this recording, with his solicitor, but we would not see the recording of his police interview.

Putting the explicit details in to words was torturous but it was important to me and the case that this was accurate, so I had to use the proper words. I prayed for strength and thought about this psalm:

"When I called you answered me, you greatly emboldened me." Psalm 138:3 *(NIV)*. Several hours later I left the room, exhausted.

We were advised not to tell our siblings that we had reported the crimes as they might incriminate themselves by trying to protect Wayne from being arrested. This was to protect them and the case.

Zoe and I went to the pub. A friend of mine was there but I pretended I hadn't seen her as I was so drained I couldn't even face friends.

We were initially appointed a support worker but my worker left after a couple of weeks as she got another job. We were also advised to seek counselling support to help us through Rape Crisis or ISAS. I self-referred to ISAS again but there was a long waiting list.

I didn't take much notice of the talk on TV of the forthcoming football World Cup coverage. Until, that was, we became concerned that nothing had been done with our statements. Weeks went by. The police told us that World Cup season was, sadly, also known by their domestic abuse team as 'Wife Battering' season as domestic abuse peaks during these tournaments. Our non-recent case was less of a priority. We understood this but the waiting was agony.

I went on holiday with Ed, our children and their partners and whilst we were away, I felt drawn to read a certain section of books in the Bible from Romans through to 2 Thessalonians. Each day I read a section whilst looking out to sea and found my strength being returned to me through reading scriptures such as Philippians 4 verse13 (NIV):

"I can do all things through Christ who strengthens me," and

"If God is for us, who can be against us?" Romans 8 verse 31 (NIV)

After we returned from holiday, we got the call: Wayne had been arrested and taken to the police station. This was a relief. We knew his health wasn't great but he was more than capable of travelling in a car and talking, which apparently, he did.

David got involved now; he and his girlfriend rang the police 'aggressively' objecting to Wayne being interviewed. The police described them as 'obstructive.'

Our siblings and our mum all knew that us reporting was a possibility and Gary had encouraged us to report Wayne, but none of them were supporting or choosing us now.

After Wayne was interviewed the officers told us that he 'went on-and-on' in his interview, much to their frustration. In summarising, they said he had told them we had been mentally damaged by our own father and therefore making the charges up. Over the years this was his first threat. He had apparently expressed his confidence that our mother would support him in his statement.

Zoe and I feared he would ask someone else to fulfil his second threat; to kill us. We were proactively more vigilant and asked our children to be too. Our children were immensely supportive but bewildered by our mum and siblings' lack of compassion towards Zoe, me, and them.

My husband gave a statement about when, where and what I told him about the abuse.

Zoe's ex-husband was interviewed. On one occasion, when Zoe bought her first house and Geoff, Ed and I were there helping, Wayne scaled the six-foot fence and stormed in aggressively. We all flew out of the back door. Geoff relayed this, the car chases, the tacks on his drive and more in his statement.

My doctor gave a statement detailing when I had told her about the abuse and about the counsellors, she had referred me to.

My school friend Sally rang me when the officer was at her house. Sally asked me:

"Nel what shall I say? I can't remember that much?" I asked her what she could remember. She said she remembered me telling her about the girl at the 18th birthday party and that I had told her he'd tried it on with me but most of all she could remember him stalking me. I told her to just tell the police officer what she remembered. It was explained to us that these 'early disclosures' over the years offer good evidence to support the case.

Then, one-by-one our siblings were interviewed by the police. I told the police that David wouldn't lie. He did. He said he knew nothing about the abuse. I felt sad for him and for us.

I knew Gary would go on a bit in an attempt to fog them but I hoped he would tell them about the abuse he had witnessed. He didn't. He said he knew nothing about it. I was so disappointed.

Trish who had feared she 'would be next,' told the police she knew nothing of the abuse. My heart sank.

The officer then reported that Alison's statement:

"did not support you or otherwise". I screamed inside 'no Alison, not you too!'

When it came to our mum's turn, the interviewing officer asked me if we wanted her to be interviewed, in view of her health. I paused for a moment as I thought this could be an opportunity for her to show her support and love for us, but I quickly relented and said:

"No, no of course not, don't bother her." It turned out that she wanted to be interviewed as she felt she might be implicated and she gave a ten-page statement, after which the officer told us:

"Her statement does not support you." It supported Wayne. This felt like a fist to my stomach. With each report back from the police something inside me seemed to shut down. I suppose I always knew deep down that my mum and siblings may stand with Wayne but I hoped they would choose the line of truth.

'Enough!' Came the voice from inside me. Enough of being betrayed, time-after-time by my mum and now by her children too. I was comforted by Psalm 27 verse 10 (NIV):

"Though my father and mother forsake me, the Lord will receive me."

The police said there was evidence of collaboration between our siblings and Mum and there was evidence that they did know about the abuse, therefore they could have left themselves open to being charged with perjury in court. After each interview the police stressed that this did not undermine the case as the evidence against Wayne was so strong. The police doctor assessed Wayne as being fit for arrest but said that further interviews would need to be done at his home.

In relation to our mum and siblings response one person said something to me about people having grey areas on these issues. I said I was very open to grey areas but could not get my head around people lying to the police as being a grey area. I discussed grey areas with Ed that night and he reassured me that lying to the police was a black and white matter. I still struggled to get to sleep. I was re-assured when I turned UCB (United Christian Broadcasters) radio *Ref 6.1* on the next morning and the person speaking said:

"You may think there are grey areas in life but the Lord despises a lying witness and loves those who speak the truth." There are many Bible verses on speaking the truth. I think this was inspired by Proverbs 12 verse 22.

Everything was happening so very slowly that we became fearful that Wayne would not be charged. Differing opinions left us feeling very uncertain so I emailed the national Crown Prosecution Service (CPS) for advice on the law. Was he too old or too ill? They responded saying age was not relevant and that his health would be assessed nearer the court case.

A couple of weeks later we were summoned to the local police station by a senior officer. The CPS had sent the local station copies of my email and their reply. I was told in no uncertain terms that I should not contact the CPS (not even the national CPS), nor anyone else, as it may weaken the case. I considered myself properly reprimanded!

We were told we would get to speak to a barrister before the court case and read all the written statements then. Wayne would have a solicitor to defend him and an intermediary to assist him in court. He would have a health assessment nearer the time when a medical expert would determine his fitness to stand. His health would be considered when sentencing. The option of video links was also discussed, for him and for us.

Throughout the process we did not have a solicitor. My support worker had left for another job, so I had no support. I thought of seeking private legal advice, of employing a private detective to trace Wayne's first wife, his mistress and the foster children but I daren't as we did not want to do anything to jeopardise the case. We felt abandoned; but we just had to wait.

Every morning I hoped Alison would contact us to reassure us that she would always choose us and she would see that the stance the family had taken was wrong. I could understand their response as a knee-jerk reaction, but weeks down the line I was sure their consciences would bring them to their senses. However, nothing came, from any of them. Eventually the police did get in touch to tell us that the Crown Prosecution Services (CPS) were taking Wayne to court and they were: "Confident of a conviction."

References

6.0 The National Association for People Abused in Childhood 0808 801 0331 www.napac.org.uk

6.1 United Christian Broadcasters Prayer Line 01782 36 3000 / Republic of Ireland 1890 940 300 www.ucb.co.uk

6.2 Williams M, contributing writer, Our Daily Bread devotional, 2007- current Discovery Ministries www.odb.org

6.3 From Report to Court - Home Office report www.rapecrisis.org.uk

"I lift up my eyes to the hills— where does my help come from? My help comes from the LORD,

the maker of heaven and earth."

Psalm 121 verse 1 (NIV).

My Story – Adulthood -Chapter 7

Comfort and coping

During the case, comfort came in all sorts of ways. Encouraging words came from friends (not all knew what our storm was, only that we were in one) and we had the unwavering support of our children, our husbands, our friends and our church leaders. Our children and Zoe's children stood firmly with us. They were all in despair that their nan, aunties and uncles had betrayed us and them, as we had all been so close.

Zoe posted me copies of letters she had just found that Dad had sent after we had been snatched from him. In the early 1970s, despite being in deep depression, he had written to The Houses of Parliament and to the County Council explaining that we had been snatched from him and that he had legal custody of us but no funds or legal aid available to him to fight for our return. He wrote of his concern that we would be being used to work in our mum's businesses and to look after Wayne and Mum's other children. He also wrote that he feared we would be afraid to speak up, that we were being stopped from writing to him and that they would set us against him. That same month he had written to us to ask to see us. I was never shown this letter by my mum, or asked if I wanted to see my dad. Dad's letters and the replies made sad reading but offered some comfort in that it showed that he had tried to help us.

The months before, during and after reporting were difficult and I prayed a lot. Scriptures sent by friends reminded me to stay close to God, such as:

"I will take refuge in the shadow of your wings until the disaster has passed." Psalm 57 verse 1 (NIV).

God spoke to me through friends, through the Bible, through church sermons, via Christian TV and radio and through songs, which all reminded me that he is a living God. I could see God's presence in all of his creation. I also heard from God for my friends, who were facing their own challenges. One friend was in hospital for months, in a desperate state. I prayed for her and visited her but we stayed in more regular contact by text. One day I felt prompted to send her a verse from the Bible, which I did not understand, (abridged from Genesis 41 verse 52 RSV):

"The name of the second he called Ephraim, for God has made me fruitful in the land of my affliction." My friend replied to say that the nurse looking after her that day was called Ephraim! She took comfort from this and is now home with her family and although not 100% recovered, she is well.

It was on a cold autumn morning, whilst we were still awaiting news of the court date, that we received the news that Wayne had died.

The police explained his crimes were classed as detected but the investigation would be discontinued due to his death. Initially I felt numb, then feelings of relief and anger surfaced. I was exhausted. He died a guilty man and I prayed for forgiveness, again. I let our friends know what had happened. Zoe and I were inundated with messages of support. Zoe said she thought she'd sleep for 100 years as she felt:

"Shell-shocked, shaky, stunned, relieved, lighter."

The police officers who interviewed us thanked us for our efforts to see some justice done and re-assured us that we were believed and that the CPS would have prosecuted Wayne.

The week after Wayne's death we visited the Crown Prosecution Services (CPS) Lawyer who had prepared the court case. One of the police officers, who took our original statements and arrested Wayne, drove us there. She said that she felt Wayne could have apologised but she said that he clearly wasn't sorry. She reminded us that the police were neutral and whilst he had a solicitor throughout the process, we only had a support worker and only for part of the time. She acknowledged that Wayne had had more protection and care than us. The CPS Lawyer told us:

"I have no doubt of his guilt, I wanted to prosecute him and I was confident of a conviction." She said that in going through the reporting process she felt we had had 'counselling-by-fire' but she hoped we would get some release and relief knowing that Wayne would have been prosecuted.

When I said I felt that reporting non-recent sexual abuse crimes was valuable in challenging the pattern of perpetrators for future generations she looked knowingly at her assistant and they both nodded in agreement.

The CPS Lawyer said she could tell there had been collaboration amongst our siblings and Mum in their statements. She recognised that our family had deserted us and she told us to hold our heads up high.

The CPS followed this up with a letter confirming that Wayne would have been prosecuted and the police sent letters to us stating that his crimes were classed as detected and only discontinued due to his death. Similar cases going through the courts around the time that Wayne would have been in court, attracted substantial prison sentences (see second part of book on 'What is Being Done?')

I needed God's peace around me to come to terms with it all and I found comfort in statements such as that of the early 20th century author and evangelist, Oswald Chambers who said:

"There will come one day a personal and direct touch from God when every tear and perplexity, every oppression and distress, every suffering and pain, every wrong and injustice will have a complete and ample and overwhelming explanation." *Ref 7.2*

I was partly relieved that Wayne had died as we would not have to go to court now. I thought the suffering would be over. It wasn't over. It was torturous, going over and over it all in my mind, then, soon after Wayne's death Trish emailed me with two pages of insults and accusations. Her response was painful and I was bewildered as we had cared for her whilst suffering Wayne's abuse and its consequences.

I reflected that I had wanted Wayne to be accountable and for his crimes to be acknowledged, and for him to have a chance to apologise. I prayed for God's grace to continue in forgiveness.

Around this time my ISAS referral came through and I was assigned to an amazing lady called Polly. Polly was such a support as I talked through my struggles with her.

Happy times threaded through unhappy ones. Over a year, we had 12 major life events, including both our daughters getting married, so I drew near to God for strength and he really did draw near to me. A happy day was when Ed and I renewed our marriage vows at our new church. Zoe was there with her new husband Marcus, which made our day. Ed's family, our church friends and my friend Marie were there too. Our daughter Amy sang: 'Into your Hands I Commit Again,' *Ref 7.5* Marie cried all the way through! It was a beautiful service and gave me some release from the pain of our wedding day.

Around this time Alison wrote to me saying she thought our relationship was worth a meeting and that we had made incorrect assumptions about her. She was right; our relationship was worth a meeting; I hoped we had made incorrect assumptions and I was optimistic that she would say something like:

113

'Oh, Nel I didn't know what to do, Oliver was so horrified and I just froze, I'm so sorry.' So, we arranged to meet at a local country park. Polly, my counsellor, had a more realistic view and said:

"Your sister will be coming with some monkeys on her back; her own and some the rest of the family have given her. She will want you to take these monkeys. Give them back to her and if she won't take them tell her to throw them away." Polly had many helpful metaphors and analogies; what a Godsend Polly was!

Walking towards Alison I felt only love. We hugged each other but we had barely walked out of the car park before Alison said:

"I have to tell you that I have consulted the rest of the family and we all stand by our actions." My heart sank but I stayed and we walked around the park and went over the case.

I spoke about the Manic Street-Porters' song (I was mixing The Manic Street Preachers up with Janet Street- Porter I think!) This made us laugh as I always got bands' names mixed up. But when I spoke seriously about the lyrics of the band's song and how our action in reporting could help protect the next generation, if only as a deterrent, I could see Alison was struggling to disagree with the lyrics:

"If you tolerate this then your children will be next." Ref 7.1

Alison said that the police officer interviewing her had got the names and some facts mixed up and that she offered some information when this happened but Polly was right; there were a lot of 'monkeys' from the family. I had to bat them off as we went over the case and I

114

encouraged Alison to throw them away. It seemed clear to me that they were all held under Wayne and Mum's grooming still.

Three hours later I left the park exhausted, sad, and no further forward. Our children were relieved to hear from me but they were very sad too. Ed said that disappointment was not a strong enough word for how he felt.

I loved my siblings. I hated what Wayne had done and that he had been allowed to carry out his third threat – to split the family up. I hated that the survivors were being criticised for finally finding the strength to speak out against the perpetrator. Our mum and siblings didn't seem to realise, or want to realise, how very hurt we were; they had had to tell themselves certain things to justify standing with Wayne. These were not compatible with the truth. My thoughts took me to the Bible:

"Stand firm, then, and do not let yourselves be burdened again by a yoke of slavery." Galatians 5 verse 1 (NIV).

I looked at the three little bridesmaids' dresses hanging in my wardrobe ready for our daughter Amy's summer wedding. There should have been a fourth dress for Alison's little girl, but any hope of us reuniting after our meeting, and having a normal wedding with them all there had gone.

I had to park my sadness about my mum and siblings so I could focus on Amy's wedding. The night before, as we pulled up in the church car park, heavy storms including thunder and lightning, engulfed the area. As we walked towards the building a huge rainbow appeared over the whole church. I took a photograph. The 'Noah' song from our children's Sunday School days echoed in my mind, which ends: "whenever you see a rainbow, remember God is love." *Ref 7.3* People in raincoats and wellington boots were running in and out of the church. We walked in ready to prepare the wedding room but were met by a very moving scene; lots of people were hanging bunting, setting up the band, laying tables and arranging flowers, like the Disney creatures in Cinderella. The support was overwhelming and I held back a tear. The rain forecast for the wedding day was replaced by sunshine so the hog roast and live music were enjoyed by the 300 guests outside. The evening band kept the dance floor full and the helpers stayed to wave the happy couple off and to help us clear up. With few of my own family there our church family helped fill that gap. I fell asleep that night praying:

"Thank you, thank you, thank you, thank you God," over and over.

A few months later we held a similar-sized fantastic Christmas wedding for Rebecca, on a frosty wintery day with the same amazing support from our church family. Again, I fell asleep that night praying:

"Thank you, thank you, thank you, thank you God," over and over.

It was after the weddings were over and before Christmas that I decided I needed to say goodbye to my wider family properly. I could not see how we could sit around the table laughing and joking with them all, as we had done before, knowing they had betrayed us, showed no signs of regret and made no attempt to make things right. I sent Christmas cards wishing them peace, expressing my sadness and saying goodbye.

Feelings of loss and an ache, similar to the pain I had experienced when we were snatched from Dad and Nan, filled my heart.

It was around this time that Jimmy Savile died. A tribute programme was aired by the BBC a few days after his death. Stories about an axed BBC investigation into him appeared in the newspapers as did information about his abuse of children. ITV exposed him as a prolific paedophile. The floodgates opened and the media has consistently reported on thousands of non-recent sex abuse cases since then and many investigations and reviews have been, and are being, carried out.

Living with an abuser for nearly ten of my formative years was tough. But I learnt things that have been useful in my life; it is hard to keep the good but discard the bad in these areas. It is a battle between wanting to be rid of anything that reminds me of the horror, whilst also valuing the good skills passed on. Constantly questioning what to hold on to and what to let go of is exhausting.

I have had to make myself re-think associations with Wayne such as accents and behaviours. There are associations (eg words, smells, music etc) that can trigger unwelcome memories but I capture these thoughts. This is another ongoing, tiring process.

During the year we reported the abuse to the police, and even more so afterwards I found it impossible to keep going for a whole day without sleeping. My body ached from head to toe. I couldn't think straight and felt as if I was in a fog. When I gave up alcohol for Lent, I thought I would feel better but I felt worse so I went to the doctor and was diagnosed with fibromyalgia, which is similar to chronic fatigue syndrome.

I subsequently attended the Freedom in Christ Ref 5.2 course again and this time I prayed the forgiveness prayer over myself, my siblings and my mum. I kept praying for a healthy relationship for us all. Sadly, this did not evolve and on a cold, sunny winter's day the news of Mum's death came, almost six years on from our estrangement. I mourned the mum I didn't have as well as the one I did. I was also mindful of my siblings' grief. It says in the Bible that love is stronger than death and I had to sift the love that was between us and try to save this. I decided to take the good and throw the rest away. I prayed for forgiveness for my mum again. I believed my mum would want me to be happy and I decided to go with that thought.

Zoe and I went to our mum's funeral, with our husbands, but we sat at the back and left by the back door.

I believe in an all-powerful, loving and eternal God and that giving my family to God, in prayer, is a much more effective choice than holding bitterness. On a daily basis I choose not to recall misdeeds and counselling has helped with this. I am recalling them for this book of course, to try to help others, but will continue to ask for God's grace to forgive. What happened to me affected me, but it did not define me; my character and what God says about me defines me – and all of us. I choose to focus on the lovely, pure, noble, admirable and right things as suggested in Philippians 4 verse 8. I direct my mind towards these things regularly. I leave room for the new thing, promised to us in Isaiah 43 verse19 (NIV), which starts:

"See I am doing a new thing." The more I do this, the more the memories soften.

I reached the stage of just wanting to see Alison, regardless of our differences; I had heard she had another baby. I prayed God would show me the way forward; we eventually met up in 2017 and have now met for lunch several times. The love and the humour between us are as strong as ever. It is only when we get on to the subject of her dad or the case that things go awry.

Zoe and our children were considering entering back into a relationship with Alison but felt they needed some sort of apology or acknowledgement. Their door was and is open for this. But offering this as a way forward was met with anger. Sorry really does seem to be the hardest word. Maybe I was over-reaching in trying to restore Alison's relationship with Zoe and our children.

I am thankful that I lived the first seven years of my life with Dad and Nan. I thank God for the judge who, against the thinking of that era, awarded Dad custody of us as babies. I am grateful that I had and have a loving, constant-sibling in Zoe and I am blessed to have found my faith and focus in Jesus. I am also truly appreciative of my husband and our wonderful family, friends and supportive church family. I recognise that some survivors have not had such things to be thankful for. Whilst I can't share all of these with them, I can share my faith in Jesus and I invite them to join me in this (see Salvation Prayer at the end of the resources pages).

I have recently had prayer ministry with a lovely lady at our church, who is trained and experienced in the 'Immanuel Approach prayer ministry' [Ref 7.6] Many things were prayed over, including prayers for release for my siblings. These prayer sessions helped me to trust, even more, in Jesus' love and His presence with me.

My faith in God continues to grow as I learn about and experience the wonders of his love every day. The song 'You're an Overcomer', [Ref 7.4] has encouraged me to see myself as just that.

Physically I suffer from several health issues, which may be attributable to the abuse. I live my life around these. My faith has helped me immensely and thankfully I don't take drugs or smoke. I am performance driven; I can be a bit of a day-dreamer and I enjoy a little too much wine and comfort food!

Spiritually, through my faith in Jesus, I feel whole. I see my future, and the future of all survivors, as being full of hope, purpose and love.

It is healthy to feel angry about these crimes. The Bible tells us to: *"Hate what is evil; cling to what is good."* Romans 12 verse 9 (NIV). And it is natural to feel angry about injustices but I am leaning in to the supernatural in Jesus by choosing not to be bitter and not to act on my anger in a way that is wrong, from God's perspective. I prayed God would take the memories and torture of these from me so I could move on but instead he gave me the strength and help to deal with them, to soften them and to use them to try to help release others – so that we can all **move forward.**

Last Christmas I revisited the hotel where we lived with Wayne and Mum. I sat outside in the car with Ed and shed a few tears as I tried to reclaim some of the happier moments there. The saddest thing was realising it could all have been happy; it could have been a good upbringing.

I am planning to write more books, poems and songs as well as to enjoy being with my husband, expanding family and all my lovely friends. I thank God that I am blessed with being able to give and receive lots of hugs and love. I have another plan too; to take a risk and potentially open myself up to being hurt again. I said to God:

"I have totally forgiven my family, I know I have as I pray blessings over their lives and I would give them a kidney if they needed it, or go to them if they needed me." I heard God, in my heart, saying;

"They don't need your kidney; they need your love; they need my love." So, my plan is to reach out to each of my siblings and maybe offer to meet up, if they want to. I am praying about the right time and way to offer this and praying that I will be able to view them through God's eyes. We will have to 'agree-to-differ' about Wayne and not discuss him or the court case, but I hope we can find a way forward otherwise. As adults, I hope and pray they will break free from Wayne's grooming.

My greatest achievement, and that of many survivors, is that I have broken the pattern for the next generation. Through my Christian faith and conviction, I have been able to be a responsible, and hopefully fun, parent and grandparent. Our children say that they had a wonderful childhood and all have good professional and family lives now. For me this is where the victory is; I thank God for it, as 1 Corinthians 15:57 (NIV) says:

"But thanks be to God! He gives us the victory through our Lord Jesus Christ."
As for having a normal life, I don't think there is such a thing. We can only do our best with the cards we are dealt, whilst embracing what God says about us and how he values us. My faith inspires me to aspire for an exceptional life. Those who are fighting to overcome trauma are exceptional. So – an exceptional life, lived for God's glory? I'll take that over normal any day!

CONCLUSIONS:

What I struggle to accept more than anything is that similar abuses of children are happening **now.** I really don't want that to be true, but it is. This has motivated me to finish this book; as a voice for past, present and future generations of children. I hope to contribute to what it says in Genesis 50 verse 20:

"You intended to harm me, but God intended it for good to accomplish what is now being done, the saving of many lives."

I hope you will be encouraged to show even more love and kindness to children and compassion to other survivors and to yourself. And that you will be even more alert to keeping children safe.

Some readers may feel disappointed that this story does not end with Wayne being convicted; that justice was not meted. Whilst many do get convicted and imprisoned, in reality many perpetrators don't; where the crime goes unreported or the police don't pursue it or the CPS don't take the case. Sometimes the perpetrator dies before they get to court, or they are found not guilty. Where the crime is reported the victims of abuse have at least been acknowledged and had the chance to seek justice, whilst the perpetrator has had a chance to be sorry. In all instances, reported or not, I believe this is not the end of the story; God will take it from here; peace will come.

In my introduction I said that it seemed to me that my family was the only one suffering. I also mention in my story that the other girls at school seemed to be from lovely, normal families. Recently one of these school friends told me that her family had serious domestic abuse issues, one told me of her strained relationship with her mum and it came to light that another suffered sexual abuse as a child.
Lots of our peers are likely to be suffering the consequences of child sexual abuse and even more live with the aftermath of domestic abuse - **so let's be kind to each other and be gentle with ourselves.**

References

7.1 If You Tolerate This, sung by The Manic Street Preachers, (by Jones N, Dean Radford J and Moore S,1998).

7.2 As cited in Oswald Chambers (1874-1917): Abandoned to God (Mc Casland D 1993 Part 22).

7.3 Mr Noah and The Ark Cd Track 1 (Mr Noah Built an Ark, Fishy Music).

7.4 'You're an Overcomer', sung by Mandisa (2013, Glover B, Stevens CE and Garcia DA)

7.5 Into your Hands I Commit Again by Hillsong (Hillsong 2010)

7.6 Immanuel Approach Prayer Ministry www.immanuelapproach.com

"Revenge happens in one day.

Forgiveness is a whole life process."

Elona Prroj, UCB Word for Today [Ref 8.0]

My Research and Understanding - Chapter 8

What is forgiveness?

The person in need of forgiveness may not feel they need or want forgiveness or they may not be around anymore, but it is still possible to forgive them by handing them over to God and asking him to do it for you. This is what Jesus did, when he was being crucified and said:

"Father forgive them, for they do not know what they are doing." Luke 23 verse 34 (NIV). All true forgiveness is of God and we can ask for divine intervention. When we put our 'self' to one side things change, including our heart.

I dislike the 'forgive-and-forget' phrase as unless we get dementia (and we don't want that) we can't physically forget. Many survivors have experiences that trigger unwanted flashbacks; which can be more like re-living the trauma than remembering it.

One of the ways I have come to terms with forgiveness is to break the word down into <u>for</u> and <u>give</u>. To <u>for-give</u> a person is to <u>give</u> something to someone be<u>fore</u> they have done anything to deserve it, and to do so graciously and/or to: <u>give</u> them to God <u>for</u> Him to issue grace*. Trust is needed so forgiveness does not always mean relationship, where there is toxicity.

Repentance (or being sorry) is turning away from what is wrong, and towards what is good. Jesus invites us to open the door of our heart to him and to repent; to come into a loving relationship with him. We have all done things that fall short of Jesus' example and this is our own chance to be sorry.

When I read of the horrors some survivors have suffered, I empathise with the desire for revenge and the inability to forgive, especially as many of these survivors have had little or no help with their healing. I think about how Jesus wept over his friend (John 1 verse 35), over a city (John 2 verse 34) and during trials and suffering (Hebrews 5 verse 7) and I am confident he would weep with and for children who are abused.

On forgiving his son Stephen's killer Robin Oake, said:

"I cannot say it was an easy decision; forgiveness isn't natural when such a desperate tragedy happens in a family...... yet I have learnt that bitterness, hatred, revenge and a never-to-be-forgiven attitude are not the answer... I believe that my forgiveness shouldn't preclude the police and the courts from meting out just punishment." *Ref 8.1*

The Bible also tells us that God chooses to remember his people's sins no more (Hebrews 8) and in the Lord's prayer we ask God to forgive us as we forgive others (Matthew 6 verses 9-13). Isaiah 43 v 18 encourages us not to dwell on the past but to allow God to do something new in our lives. I focus on making today the best it can be and put energy into the future as a better way to forget – or to get be<u>fore</u> it. I make a daily choice to forgive; I do not want to carry the burden of unforgiveness.

In his book, 'Total Forgiveness', RT Kendall describes his commitment to forgive a major hurt as a 'life-sentence', but goes on to talk about the anointing and blessing that comes when you totally forgive. *Ref 8.2*

FORGIVENESS table by Nel:		
IS	IS NOT	NEEDS
A chance to be sorry	Revenge	Patience with self & others
Ongoing & can be complex	Always a one-off event	*Grace
Naming the offence	Calling a guilty person innocent	Remorse and sorrowfulness
Acknowledging happenings	Denying what happened	Repentance
Acknowledging the effects	Carrying another person's shame	Acknowledgement of the crime
Compatible with justice	Avoiding justice and the courts	Wisdom, mercy and truth
Giving more than deserved	Denial / sweeping a crime under the carpet	*Grace and **compassion
Becoming strong in God	Insurance against future hurts	*Grace, relief and redemption.
Respecting self and others	Suffering in toxic relationships	Separation if toxicity persists
*Grace - unearned favour, kindness, spiritual reward. Eg Jesus dying for us **Compassion –responding to others' suffering. Eg Jesus was compassionate towards the 'helpless' in Matthew 9:36		

Elona Prroj said of her husband Tani's murder in 2010 (a revenge killing as part of a so-called blood feud):

"Sometimes we think forgiveness happens in one day, but it is the opposite, revenge happens in one day. Forgiveness is a whole life process. Every morning I wake up and ask God for the strength and grace to forgive." *Ref 8.0*

It is the Holy Spirit's place to convict people of their need for forgiveness but those who don't want forgiveness are missing out on the peace that comes with this. Those who feel they have escaped justice may want to reconsider their position after reading Galatians 6 verse 7 (NIV):

"Do not be deceived: God cannot be mocked. A man reaps what he sows". Whilst Nahum 1 verse 3 (NIV) states:

"The Lord is slow to anger but great in power; the Lord will not leave the guilty unpunished."

Saying sorry

Some of the ingredients for an apology seem to be: taking responsibility for and acknowledging what went wrong, expressing regret, actually saying sorry, offering to put things right or offering to recompense the other person and asking for their forgiveness. When the prodigal son returned home after hurting his father, he was remorseful and offered to work as a servant. His actions spoke louder than words.

Trust is the key so even where a genuine apology is accepted there is no guarantee of an ongoing relationship, where trust has been badly eroded.

Avid confessor

An abuser may fall into the pattern of being an avid confessor to try to minimise their crime and disarm the victim of domestic abuse by saying sorry. Where actions do not match words saying sorry is worthless. Where a victim of domestic abuse receives repeated apologies and promises of better behaviour but then the abuse continues, the trust is eroded. Here an apology holds little or no value.

Self-Control

"The fruit of the spirit is love, joy, peace, forbearance, kindness, goodness, faithfulness, gentleness and self-control. Against such things there is no law." Galatians 5 verses 22-23 (NIV). God gave us all free will. He does not control us and does not want us to control others or be controlled by others, each having self-control.

References

8.0 Elona Prroj, United Christian Broadcasters, Word for Today, 2016/2017 issue.

8.1 Oake R, Father Forgive 2008, Authentic Media

8.2 Kendall RT, Total Forgiveness, 2001, updated version 2020, RT Kendall Ministries, rtkendallministries.com

"He has sent me to bind up the broken-hearted, to proclaim freedom for the captives and release from darkness for the prisoners ... to bestow on them a crown of beauty instead of ashes, the oil of joy instead of mourning, and a garment of praise instead of a spirit of despair."

Abridged from Isaiah 61 verses 1-3 (NIV)

My research and understanding - Chapter 9

Issues around abuse

I am not a professional nor am I medically qualified (please speak to your doctor or a professional and refer to the resources page to get support). We all respond differently so please ignore anything that doesn't line up with how you feel. Recommended books, by professionals, are on the resources page. For ease referencing is included in each paragraph. These are observations from my research as a survivor:

The Law

Lifelong anonymity

Victims of sexual assault have the right to be and to stay anonymous for life, under The Sex Offences Act (www.cps.gov.uk). Publishers in the UK are regulated by The Independent Press Standards Authority (www.ipso.org) and have to abide by the rules in The Editors' Code of Practice. Code 11 says the press **must not identify** victims of sexual assault or publish material likely to contribute to such identification unless there is adequate justification and they are legally free to do so. It is rare and exceptional for justification to be found. Victims can give up their right to anonymity where they choose to.

Perpetrator usually known to the victim

According to the Crown Prosecution sex attack victims usually know their attacker. See *CPS Rape and Sexual Offences - Chapter 21: Societal Myths*

Rape Crisis say 90% of victims know their attacker, with only 10% of perpetrators being 'strangers'. *See www.rapecrisis.org Myths versus Realities.*

Age of Consent

The age of consent (the legal age to have sex) in the UK is 16 years-old. According to NSPCC these laws are to protect children from abuse or exploitation, rather than to prosecute under-16s who mutually participate in consenting sexual activity. The law also says that anyone under the age of 13 can never legally give consent. It is also illegal to take, show or distribute indecent photographs of a child; to pay for or arrange sexual services of a child and it is illegal for a person in a position of trust (eg teacher) to engage in sexual activity with anyone under the age of 18 who is in the care of their organisation. See Legal Definitions at www.nspcc.org

Paedophile

A paedophile is someone who is sexually interested in children. Adults who sexually abuse children are paedophiles. There are other definitions breaking down the ages of children they abuse but this is the overall description used. The Crown Prosecution Services www.cps.gov.uk details the legislation.

How a case is pursued

The police need evidence to pursue a case and the Crown Prosecution Services (CPS) will not take a case without sufficient evidence. Evidence can include direct statements, physical evidence, witness statements and a variety of other types of evidence. See www.cps.gov.uk

Criminal and civil law

Criminal law in the UK requires a defendant to be proved guilty 'beyond reasonable doubt.' Civil law looks at the 'balance of probability.' It is more complex than this and each case is unique. Do take legal advice.

Not guilty or innocent?

A court can only find a perpetrator 'guilty' or 'not guilty' based on the evidence before them. They do not pronounce someone innocent. A perpetrator's crime is theirs, whatever the court finds.

Sentencing

The court applies the law that was in place at the time of the crime. Harsher sentences are available to courts for current, similar crimes. Consideration seems to be given to how remorseful (sorry) a criminal is for their crime.

The Domestic Violence Disclosure Scheme (DVDs) - DV is now referred to as Domestic Abuse.

In 2014 The DVD Scheme, known as Clare's Law, was extended to police forces across England and Wales. This allows police to disclose details, to individuals (or a concerned family member or friend), in confidence, of their partner's abusive past. Call 101 to request a DVD form. www.gov.uk

The Domestic Violence Bill 2018 - DV is now referred to as Domestic Abuse.
As well as improving DVDs, this bill gives greater priority to children, prevents perpetrators cross-examining their victims in family courts and creates an assumption that victims of domestic abuse and abuse will automatically be entitled to special measures in court such as video-linked interviews or giving evidence from behind a screen. This bill also presented a new definition of domestic abuse and proposed a Domestic Abuse Commissioner be appointed. Domestic abuse is now treated as a crime by the police who have specially trained officers and Domestic Abuse Units to deal with perpetrators. www.gov.uk

Restorative justice
"Restorative justice gives victims the chance to tell offenders the real impact of their crime, get answers to their questions and get an apology." This is part of the description of restorative justice at www.gov.uk with more information and support available at www.victimsupport.org.uk. Safety of the victim is paramount.

Abuse and its effects

Statistics

More than one-in-seven adults in the UK are survivors of some form of child sexual abuse and this crime costs the UK *£3.2 billion a year. NSPCC say any figures will not include those children who don't tell anyone because they feel guilty or afraid, those who don't know who to tell and those children who may not realise they are being abused. Child abuse often goes unreported and unrecorded.

*L Radford, etal, 'Child Abuse and Neglect in the UK Today' (London: NSPCC 2011). See www.nspcc.org

The World Health Organization (WHO) estimates that a third of women worldwide have been victims of sexual violence. www.who.int

Suicide

Victims of abuse are more vulnerable to suicidal thoughts. NPCC website's report identifies the link between abuse and suicide. See www.nspcc.org

There were 6507 suicides registered in the UK in 2018 (Office of National Statistics), which was significantly higher than in 2017. See www.ons.gov.uk. The NHS Choices website www.nhs.uk states that:

"Many experts believe a number of things determine how vulnerable a person is to suicidal thinking and behaviour. These include: life history –

for example, having a traumatic experience during childhood, a history of sexual or physical abuse, or a history of parental neglect."

Maimed

I feel that someone who sexually abuses a child maims their victim as much as if they had ripped a limb off. In some cases, their crime equates to murder (the prison sentences available under current law reflect this).

Coping mechanisms

Having to hide or work-around the injury of abuse takes a lot of energy. Everyone copes differently with this. Some of the common coping mechanisms for survivors seem to be workaholism, disassociation, self-harm and 'self-medication' with alcohol, drugs, smoking, and food.

In the short-term some of these coping mechanisms are necessary, invaluable defence mechanisms and we humans are wonderfully designed to enable ourselves to adapt to cope and survive. They form part of our defences, but in the long-term some are self-harm, which may affect the individual and their family. Love, support and encouragement can help survivors learn other coping mechanisms.

Dissociative Identity Disorder (DID)

Dissociation is another trauma survival strategy. For some consciousness of feelings, sensations and memories can be limited leading to anxiety, fatigue, memory loss and difficulties managing emotions and sleep, amongst other symptoms. DID is recognised as a way of surviving childhood trauma and psychotherapy treatment can offer relief. For more information visit PODS (Positive Outcomes for Dissociative Survivors) www.pods-online.org.uk

Chronic Fatigue Syndrome (CFS)

There is some research that indicates this and similar chronic conditions such as fibromyalgia can be caused by traumatic events in childhood (see www.nhs.uk Childhood Trauma and ME)).

Post-Traumatic Stress Disorder (PTSD)

The Journal of Traumatic Stress* reported that 94 percent of women experience PTSD within two weeks of a sexual assault.

Post-traumatic stress disorder results from injury or severe shock and is a condition triggered by experiencing or witnessing something terrifying. It can include flashbacks, nightmares, severe anxiety and uncontrollable thoughts. PTSD can affect relationships and work and can lead to addictions and unhealthy choices. *Herman, Judith L, 1992 International Society for Traumatic Stress Studies www.istss.org*

Complex Post-Traumatic Stress Disorder (CPTSD)

A single event such as being in or witnessing an attack can cause PTSD. When a person is subjected to attacks or threats of attacks over a longer period this can cause Complex PTSD. The NHS website states:

"CPTSD may be diagnosed in adults or children who have repeatedly experienced traumatic events such as violence, neglect or abuse." It says this is likely to be more severe where the trauma happened early in life, was caused by a parent or carer, took place over a long period of time, where the person was alone during the trauma and where there is still contact with the person responsible for the trauma. The symptoms of CPTSD can be debilitating on many levels. See www.mind.org.uk and www.nhs.uk

Wired for fear (cited on *www.sideeffectspublicmedia.org*)

In his book, 'The Body Keeps the Score,' Bessel Van der Kolk looks at how abuse and neglect in childhood affects the brain and at how childhood trauma can lead to a person's brain being wired for fear. He says a brain that is set to feel in danger and fear as a child can be more fearful and sensitive in adulthood, which can lead to responses such as excessive shutting down, anger and unhealthy coping mechanisms.

Van der Kolk, Bessel A. The Body Keeps the Score: Brain, Mind, and Body in the Healing of Trauma. Viking, 2014.

Secondary Assault

Where a survivor has the crimes against them minimised or dismissed their experience is not validated and this can lead to the feelings of anger and depression, a sort of secondary assault.

Victim mentality

Children who are victims of abuse may feel powerless and feel that the world is not a safe place, distrusting authority and feeling shame for something which was not their fault.

Accusing someone of 'acting the victim' or having a 'victim's mentality,' is often tried as a way to silence a victim of abuse or to try to justify the abuse. It enables those complicit with the abuse or their role in protecting the abuser to continue in denial. Taking on these accusations gives power to others over the survivor's life.

However, perpetrators may try to play the 'victim card', to justify their crime.

Silent

Speaking to someone or reporting the crime can release a victim of abuse from feeling silenced; leaving them the choice of when to be silent, not silenced.

Shame

Shame is often used as a tool of abuse and is known as the 'secret-keeper,' as victims of abuse feel the message shame gives is that 'there is something wrong with me.'

Those loosely linked with the crime of abuse go to great lengths to avoid the shame; we were cast aside by our family; my sister planned to move to Australia if her father's name appeared in the newspapers; some charities prioritised the fear of the shame on the organisation above protecting the victims of abuse; a celebrity was awarded huge damages for being named as being under police investigation for this crime. Sadly, some people take their own lives. In some cases, logic seems to disappear and yet some seem to feel no shame; whilst the shame of being loosely linked to the crime seems to be recognised more than being a victim of the actual crime.

The Compass of Shame is explained in Donald Nathanson's book as being a tool which breaks down the defences someone feeling shame may exhibit as: withdrawal, avoidance, attacking self and attacking others. *'Shame & Pride' by Donald L Nathanson, 1992, on Amazon.*

Secondary victims of abuse

Whilst they don't experience the actual injury, family, friends and even professionals can experience physical and psychological symptoms on hearing about it, as a sort of vicarious trauma. Professionals are trained to deal with this. This represents another motivation to prevent this crime. See www.secondarytrauma.org.

Other related issues

Gas-lighting

Many victims of abuse are subjected to emotional abuse called 'gas-lighting'. This phrase originates from the 1938 play, Gas Light, by Patrick Hamilton, in which the husband makes his wife think she is going mad by dimming the gas lights and making her think she had imagined it. This is coercive control and is a crime.

Domestic violence (DV) - DV is now referred to as Domestic Abuse.

This includes psychological, physical, sexual, financial and emotional and other forms of abuse. Citizens' Advice Bureau describes domestic abuse as:

"Controlling, coercive or threatening behaviour, violence or abuse between people aged over 16." See www.citizenadvice.org.uk

The Office of National Statistics (ONS) lists domestic abuse as one of the most prevalent crimes in England and Wales, accounting for 33% of violent crime recorded by the police in the year to March 2018. See www.ons.gov.uk

NSPCC says witnessing or experiencing domestic abuse is a form of child abuse, causes serious harm and can indicate children are at risk from other types of abuse including physical, sexual and emotional abuse and neglect. One-in-five children have been exposed to domestic abuse. See www.nspcc.org

Professional training often describes domestic abuse as a choice, in that the person controls themselves not to hurt someone at the bus stop but allows themselves to go home and harm so-called 'loved ones.'

Grooming

NSPCC defines grooming, which can be by a stranger or someone known to them, as building:

"an emotional connection with a child to gain their trust for the purposes of sexual abuse, sexual exploitation or trafficking." This can be on-line or face-to-face and can include psychological grooming of adults and children, by trust, persuasion and manipulation. See www.nspcc.org.

Scapegoating

Scapegoating is a phrase used to describe a child who is bullied, abused and sacrificed for the sake of the rest of the family. There is much written on this subject and in relation to the golden-child (a child held up as the favoured/perfect one), which many survivors will relate to. Neither being a healthy role. The description of narcissistic parenting seems to relate to some abusers too. All worth researching.

Fight, flight or freeze

I felt bad that I froze the first time Wayne assaulted me, but this is recognised as one of the typical responses to acutely stressful situations. The heart races as the body prepares for danger and the body and mind sometimes shut down/freeze, for protection and to allow time to decide whether to fight or flee. It can take an hour to return to previous levels.

Family mutiny

I have included my family's response in my story as it seems common for families to turn on the victims of abuse. I asked some professional friends and survivors why they think this happens. They suggested:

- misplaced loyalty - anger projected on to the victim of abuse instead of the perpetrator.

- groomed or put under pressure.

- financial - bribery, reward or protecting inheritance and/or not wanting to lose perpetrator's income

- avoid being implicated (some mothers have been imprisoned for being complicit).

- shame of it being in the media and losing reputation in community, (see paragraph on shame)

- prevent other children from going into care or having the stigma around them

- disbelieve survivor or say they don't believe them as they do not know how to deal with this.

- some blame the victim of abuse for the abuse (it is never a child's fault).
- tell themselves untrue things about the victim to justify their position - cognitive dissonance (see below).

Some family members try to 'sit on the fence.' But as Desmond Tutu said:

"If you are neutral in situations of injustice, you have chosen the side of the oppressor." *(Gish, Steven. Desmond Tutu, A Biography 2004. Tutu was Chair of The South African Truth & Reconciliation, Commission, which looked into human rights abuses around apartheid. Tutu is also the author of several books on forgiveness).*

The things we tell ourselves – cognitive dissonance

Cognitive dissonance occurs when we tell ourselves things to avoid discomfort. Cognition means thought and dissonance means discord and results in inconsistent thoughts, beliefs or attitudes. Telling ourselves something often enough, can change our ideas to support a situation and avoid conflicting thoughts.

One star, accused of child abuse, repeatedly told his victims he was showing them love and that he would never hurt a child. He told them and himself this so often it became believable to them. Cognitive dissonance is unhealthy but it removes us from the reality of a situation.

Stockholm Syndrome - victim's loyalty to the perpetrator

This term came about in the 1970s after four hostages were taken captive during a bank robbery in Stockholm, Sweden. SS was used, as a description more widely after subsequent hostage situations and then extended to include domestic abuse. In these cases, victims developed trust in, sympathy for and some attachment to their captors. The key elements of SS seem to be threat, isolation, dependency, captivity and kindness. SS is different for each person and is another unhealthy, but understandable survival strategy.

Abused does not become abuser

There is no evidence to support the phrase 'the abused becomes the abuser,' yet this phrase sticks in the public's mind and punishes survivors of abuse for life. Some survivors over compensate to try to be good parents and some burn out. For me this phrase kept me from speaking about my experience for forty years for fear of being judged by others.

When a perpetrator knows they've been found out do most either deny their crime entirely or say they were abused (whether they were or not) to get a more lenient sentence? Perpetrators often appear to be sorrier for themselves for getting caught, rather than being sorry for their crimes. Perpetrators know abuse is wrong. Abuse is a choice.

Sexualised behaviour

Children who have witnessed sexualised behaviour may play this out, which can be problematic or harmful. Where they have experienced abuse, they may not realise this is harmful. With intervention and supervision this can be unlearnt and replaced with positive behaviour. NSPCC's website includes details on what is considered harmful, why this occurs and contacts for help. See www.nspcc.org. Teaching around healthy relationships and sexual behaviour in an age-appropriate way can help keep children safe.

Media coverage

In 2015 the news featured a 55-year-old man who was badly beaten by four burglars, who were collectively sentenced to 64 years in prison. His injuries were horrific and news reporters were rightly horrified. His visible injuries brought acknowledgement and strong sentences.

Child sex abuse victims are anonymous, their injuries are usually non-visible and this crime seems to attract weaker sentences. The injuries to victims of abuse are rarely highlighted. Some reporters are sensitive, but some use accusatory words about the victim and sympathetic tones towards the perpetrator. Survivors find it hard to put this crime in to words so it is no surprise that the media need help with this.

No one wants it to be true

The summer before Rolf Harris was arrested, I considered buying one of his limited-edition prints. When his crimes were aired, I was so glad I hadn't but I did experience that feeling of not wanting it to be true. He had been a lighter part of our childhood on our TV. That he had been inflicting such a heavy lifetime burden on his victims at the same time as entertaining us sickens me. This is everyone's response to child abuse though – no one wants it to be true. Those who feel this way the most are the survivors.

Victim Blaming

Blaming the victim for a crime committed against them seems to be a regular and inexplicable occurrence. One the victim can even do to themselves. This is a 'red-herring' as in all cases the criminal is to blame for the crime.

Sometimes children are uninhibited about their bodies, explorative with clothes and make-up etc and unsure where relationship boundaries are. A responsible parent or guardian respectfully directs the child as to where the proper boundaries are, in all these areas. Where the adult betrays this trust and exploits the child instead it can leave that child feeling responsible for 'encouraging' them. This is another 'red-herring' as the perpetrator is the one at fault, not the child. Victims of child abuse can be given *no* blame for the crime against them.

We were wronged

Author and academic, Martin Westlake, wrote about his experience of being abused by his scoutmaster in a Sunday Times supplement in January 2015 *, after carrying this secret for 45 years. He sacrificed his right to anonymity to 'get his ghost out' and to try to help others. In this article he said (on giving his story):

"... it's also a way for me to encourage others to step forward, not in order to hang their heads shamefacedly and say 'we were wrong' but to stand up straight, stare our society in the face and resolutely declare: 'We were wronged.'"

* Westlake M, Sunday Times My Scoutmaster Ruined My Young Life (London: The Times January 2015)

Compliant

Some victims of abuse are persuaded to be compliant; some are compliant as a way to survive and some comply as they don't realise it is abuse. Some victims carry feelings of being 'bad' for going along with abuse. The guilt always belongs to the perpetrator, never the child.

Some people love paedophiles

Wayne's photograph recently appeared on a family member's social media inviting people to love and like and comment on it. People do still love their paedophile relative; to demonstrate this so publicly is insensitive to the victims of their abuse of course.

False allegations

A friend of ours, who worked as a care worker whilst studying for a career in the medical sector, was accused of sexual assault, by a disabled male resident. Our friend was devastated. Suspended from work he struggled to carry on with his studies and to live a full life with his young family.

Police investigations followed and the agonising process went on for months. The police found no evidence. A different care worker was present at the time and the act he accused our friend of was physically impossible. Nevertheless, our friend left this job, beaten down.

It later transpired that this resident had made similar allegations about others in the past and he had made the same allegation against a co-worker, which was also being investigated. The co-worker accused, very sadly, took their own life.

The employer should have offered more protection. The police acted rightly (though the process was painfully slow). The accuser has a lot to answer for; not only to this friend and the now deceased co-worker and their family, but also to the real victims of abuse. False accusations waste police time and cast doubt over those who have genuinely suffered (who may have taken years to find the courage to come forward).

Survivors

Many support groups for victims of abuse have 'survivors' in their title; supporting those who have survived a horrendous crime.

For those who have felt suicidal, my heart breaks and I can understand someone reaching that point. Although I haven't had suicidal thoughts my fear of being killed by my stepfather was very real. There were unnerving incidences, which led us to believe he was capable of murder and we are very glad to have survived.

Fogging

When an American politician mocked an alleged victim of abuse's evidence publicly, he made the error of believing this undermined her case. Whilst non-recent abuse cases need strong evidence to support them, they do not rely on every minor detail being recalled (eg was it a red car or a blue car he picked you up in?) After all, can you remember the minor details of a whole day even one year ago? Some of the audience laughed uncomfortably at this politician's attempts to fog the issue around sexual crimes. The humiliation is the politician's for doing what many perpetrators try to do.

Police

The police we dealt with were passionate about seeing justice, but there were a few errors along the way which could have cost the case, had our perpetrator survived to attend court. I would still report this crime to

the police though and earlier if I could. I appreciate everything the
police did – thank you.

Living in fear

Abuse knows no race, religion, class, wealth or status. It happens in
many homes – from council run homes to mansions. Professionals
should not be distracted by appearances. Mum was well spoken and
Wayne could run rings around people in conversations. As children we
were under their control. Don't rely on children's reassurances, as they
may have been groomed and may be living in fear, as we were.

Offensive language and behaviour

A man announcing to a group, reading newspapers in our library (which
is in a very nice town), that the women making non-recent sexual assault
allegations:

"probably enjoyed it." The other men said nothing. I froze. I could have
expressed my disappointment at such ignorance. Realistically our best
hope is to enlighten our family and friends about the impact of these
crimes. Public education would help.

Childhood is sacred

The charity World Vision UK invites child sponsorship and it says on its
website:

"A lost toy can be replaced. A lost childhood can't. Childhood is sacred." Have perpetrators crossed a sacred line then? Here is what Jesus said about children:

"If anyone causes one of these little ones- those who believe in me- to stumble, it would be better for them to have a large millstone hung around their neck and to be drowned in the depths of the sea." Matthew 18 verse 6 (NIV).

"Let the little children come to me, and do not hinder them, for the kingdom of heaven belongs to such as these." Matthew 19 verse 14 (NIV). Jesus also spoke of children as being a gift from God and of us welcoming children in, his name, equating to welcoming him. Jesus promised to heal the broken-hearted and bind their wounds. It is the adult, not the child who has crossed the line, no child is ever to blame.

Protecting future generations

My friend asked how she could equip her daughter to protect herself, as part of a blended family. I said build her self-esteem up, talk to her about sex and other relationship issues in an age-appropriate way, and let her know you will always listen to her. Supervise in an age-appropriate way, as leaving children to their own devices, in person or on the internet, can leave them open to abuse . The NSPCC is campaigning for changes in legislation and a Code of Practice for internet providers to prevent the use of technology to facilitate abuse. www.nspcc.org

"May we teach our children that speaking out without the fear of retribution is our culture's new North Star."

Actor Laura Dern (Time's Up) [Ref 10.1]

My research and understanding - Chapter 10

What is being done?

It has taken me ten years to write this book and alongside this the last decade has seen much progress in shedding light on the crime of child abuse and its effects. I hope the next ten years and for the rest of time there is more action to eradicate this crime and to support its victims. I invite you to pray for this with me.

Here are some of the things that have happened since 2010:

The National Crime Database came into operation in 2010 to help the police link reported crimes across the forces, nationally. See www.nationalcrimeagency.gov.uk

The Victims' Commissioner role was established in 2010 to work independently, advising The Ministry of Justice and promoting the interests of victims and witnesses. See www.victimscommissioner.org.uk

In 2010 the *Oranges and Sunshine* film further exposed the scandal of the British government's Home Children programme, which forcibly emigrated around 150,000 children in the 1950s. Many suffered abuse. There are many operations and investigations into child abuse across the UK. Here are a few:

In 2011 *Operation Daybreak* was launched by Nottinghamshire Police, to investigate accusations by victims of child abuse in a children's home or in the care system linked to the home.

Operation Yew Tree was launched in October 2012 following allegations of sexual abuse committed by Jimmy Savile and other TV stars of the 70s and 80s.

In 2014 *The Rotherham Child Abuse Scandal* was investigated and found 1400 children had been sexually exploited over 16 years.

In 2014 Nottinghamshire Police launched *Operation Xeres,* a second investigation into allegations of historic child abuse at a number of different care facilities in the county.

In 2015 Notts Police launched *Operation Equinox*, which was a merger of the two previous investigations. Equinox also looked at youth groups, churches and cubs etc

In 2015 *The Independent Inquiry into Child Sexual Abuse (IICSA)* commenced its work with the Victims and Survivors' Consultative Panel, and other expert advisers, to investigate whether public bodies and other non-state institutions had taken their duty of care seriously (to protect children from sexual abuse in England and Wales). Several seminars and public inquiries were scheduled as part of the IICSA, which is due to conclude in 2020. Many of the reports from these inquiries are online now. See www.iicsa.org.uk

Spotlight the 2015 Hollywood movie about the Catholic Church's cover-up of child-molesting priests, told the true story of the Pulitzer Prize winning investigation carried out by The Boston Globe. This investigation revealed hundreds of offenders and thousands of victims of abuse.

In 2017 the Violence Against Women and Girls Service Transformation Fund (VAWG) was announced. Forty projects shared about £17m. Then Prime Minister, Theresa May, also announced plans for a major programme to bring in the Domestic Violence and Abuse Act.

In *2017 The Crown Prosecution Service declined to take on an alleged case of non-recent sexual abuse* against a celebrity, after insufficient evidence was presented to them.

Weinstein Effect 2017
In 2017 New York Time's published a story about American film producer, Harvey Weinstein and the allegations against him for sexual harassment, assaults and rape. After this sexual harassment and assault

allegations increased by 30%. This led to the phrase the 'Weinstein Effect.'

In *2017 #MeToo Movement* went viral on social media, following a call from Actress Alyssa Milano for those who had suffered sexual abuse or harassment to put '# Me Too' on their social media.

In 2018 Time's Up was launched by over 300 Hollywood celebrities to fight sexual harassment in the workplace. Time's Up was set up in response to the Weinstein effect and the # Me Too campaign.

In *2018 a Parliamentary Report on Charities* looked into allegations of sexual abuse by some charity workers and found an "overall impression of complacency verging on complicity." *Ref 10.4*

In *2018 the 'Same-Roof Rule,' was declared incompatible with human rights law* by a Court of Appeal, after a brave survivor, known only as JT challenged this rule. The rule was part of the Criminal Injuries Compensation Scheme (CICS), which discriminated against victims of abuse, abused prior to 1st October 1979 who lived in the same household as the perpetrator. Victims of the 1979 Same Roof Rule was set up as a private Facebook group and its members supported a campaign about this. On receiving compensation, one anonymous survivor, said:

"It felt like sort of a 'sorry you have been through this.' It made me feel much better."

In *2018 Britain hosted an International Safeguarding Conference*, attended by the United Nations, International Financial Institutions, CDC (the UK's Development Finance Institution) and hundreds of Non-Government Organisations (NGOs), contractors and research organisations, with donors representing 90% of global aid. All committed to global standards to prevent sexual abuse, demanding their partners adhere.

In *2018 an All-Party Parliamentary Group (APPG) Inquiry into Survivors of Childhood Sexual Abuse* was launched. All political parties, The Survivors' Trust and adult survivors are working together to come up with recommendations to improve services.

In *2018 the police focussed on prevention and detection of child sexual abuse.* Simon Bailey (National Police Chief Council's lead on child protection) stressed his commitment to working with charities such as Stopso and other perpetrators' programmes to look at several angles for the prevention and detection of this crime. (See resources pages).

In *2018 NHS England announced Lifetime Support for Victims of Sexual Assault* as part of a five-year strategy to offer lifetime support for victims of sexual assault and abuse.

In *2018 a celebrity's right to privacy was found to outweigh the BBC's right to freedom of expression* under Article 8 of the Human Rights Act, by Mr Justice Mann, following legal action against the police and BBC. Prime Minister at the time, Theresa May said:

"There may well be cases where the publication of a name enables other victims to come forward and therefore strengthen a case."

In *2018 the BBC aired the programme 'Stacey Dooley Investigates Second Chance Sex Offenders'* about restrictions on perpetrators in Florida.

In *2018 NSPCC reported the cost of child abuse in the UK is estimated to be £3.2 Billion* [Ref 10.1.1] and launched their campaign *What if I'm right?* NSPCC encourages people, with concerns about children, to ask themselves this rather than thinking: 'what if I'm wrong?' See www.nspcc.org

In *2018 Working Together to Safeguard Children* offered statutory guidance on inter-agency working to safeguard and promote the welfare of children. See www.gov.uk

2019 rehabilitation of perpetrators. A family member of a friend of mine was imprisoned for having thousands of indecent images of children on his computer. Whilst in prison there was no help on how to avoid re-offending. The probation service provided a therapy course on release.

In *2019 two celebrities launched a petition for anonymity for suspects accused of sexual crimes, until charged.* The Home Office gave a balanced response to this, acknowledging the right to privacy for the alleged perpetrator together with the right of police to release names, where necessary, to an investigation (witnesses independently reporting similar patterns bring credibility, whereas survivors may feel unable to speak up as a lone voice). The response also pointed out that there is no evidence of mass false accusations whilst there is evidence of mass under-reporting of these crimes. See *www.petition.parliament.uk/archived/petitions/247912*

In 2020 An Independent Assurance Review found Manchester's Operation Augusta had failed victims of child abuse in their area. Underfunding and cutting short the inquiry, despite 97 persons of interest being identified, saw children 'let down' by this force. Subsequently the ongoing *Operation Green Jacket inquiry* was launched to pursue these crimes. Contact opgreenjacket@gmp.police.uk with any information.

In 2020 The Domestic Abuse Bill had its second reading in The House of Commons, after which it had the committee stage amendments and third reading stage to go through there before going through the House of Lords. It is due to gain Royal Assent in 2021.

There are thousands of cases against paedophiles going through the courts but around the time we reported Wayne, *Ronald Dean* (82), from the Southampton area, was convicted of rape, indecent assaults against children and perverting the course of justice. He was jailed for 25 years. In 2012 *Keith Brown* (68) from Nottinghamshire, was jailed for 18 years. Presenter *Stuart Hall* (then 83) was sentenced to five years, in all, for indecently assaulting young girls and was stripped of his OBE in 2013. He faced further charges in 2014. In 2014 *Rolf Harris* was jailed for almost six years for 12 indecent assaults against four girls during the 1960s-1980s.

More recently: in 2018, ex-football coach *Wayne Bennell* was sentenced to 31 years in prison for abusing young boys from 1979 to 1991. In 2019 ex-football coach *Bob Higgins* was jailed for 24 years after being found guilty on 45 counts of indecently assaulting boys between 1971 – 1996.

In 2019 Chelsea Football Club apologised un-reservedly to the many young boys abused by Eddie Heath, their chief-scout in the 1970s. They set up a support and compensation scheme for the victims of abuse and committed to improvements to eliminate these 'abhorrent crimes.' There are many other football coaches listed on the BBC website as facing justice for similar crimes.

In *2019 paedophile Carl Beech was jailed for child sex offences, fraud and for perverting the course of justice* after making serious allegations against several high-profile public figures. He was jailed for 18 years. Liz Reid of the Criminal Prosecution Services (CPS) said:

"The CPS would like to make it clear that Beech's actions betray true victims, who should never be afraid of coming forward to reveal abuse." See *www.cps.gov.uk*

In 2020 Harvey Weinstein (68) was found guilty. This film producer, mentioned earlier, was sentenced to 23 years in prison for rape and sexual assault.

What can we do?

What I have been doing

I wrote letters to the media, where I felt they mishandled survivors' stories; I questioned the language of condemnation of survivors and sympathy for perpetrators by some. I have written to the Appeals Court to object to some perpetrators' lenient sentences.

I have emailed the Independent Inquiry in to Child Sexual Abuse and The Victims' Commissioner about the disparity between sentences and compensation levels and to ask that they ban the phrase 'the abused becomes the abuser.'

What can you do?

To try to help prevent this crime and/ or get help for those who have already become victims of abuse please sign-post them to the resources in this book. Listen and be supportive when someone discloses abuse to you. Acknowledge their experience without pushing them to report, have closure or move on.

When you come across communication that is unfair to survivors of abuse write to the organisation.

Let children in your care know you will always listen to them and look out for them. Do not leave them to their own devices with other children or on the internet. Be very sure of the adults you allow to care for them. Speak to them in an age appropriate way about the boundaries needed around relationships and sex (before someone else does). Bring them up with good self-esteem to help them stand up for themselves and teach them to respect others, at all levels, most particularly children and vulnerable people. Advise the authorities if other children are in danger (you can do this anonymously – see resources page). Jesus said: *"…whatever you did for one of the least of these … you did for me."* From Matthew 24 verse 40 (NIV).

Please pray for children and survivors and for this crime to be eradicated.

What can a perpetrator do?

Take responsibility for your actions and for the crime. At the very least, be sorry. Please find a way to show some remorse and turn from this most horrific crime. Seek advice on how to do this as it could be harmful to the victim of abuse to approach them directly (see resources page). Turn yourself in to the police, get support and commit to never re-offending

What can a perpetrator's family do?

Acknowledge the crime. Don't minimise it in any way. If you have protected the perpetrator (either from the law or from the shame of this crime) please, at the very least, be sorry.

Report the crime, if it hasn't been reported. Get counselling support for yourself (see resources pages) and pass this book on to the survivor for them to get the support they need via the resources' pages.

What can a church do?

Be Trauma-Informed. In his book, 'Breakthrough. The Art of Surviving,' [Ref 10.2] Psychotherapist, Ordained Minister and Survivor Giles D Lascelle talks about the importance of training and education in churches around the area of trauma. As well as offering an understanding of the issues around trauma and abuse Giles stresses the need to be trauma-informed. Giles leads the Breakthrough charity, offering training in this area of expertise to church leaders at all levels. Visit www.traumabreakthrough.org to get your church trauma-informed training and/or to order this book for your church leaders and members to read.

What can a survivor do?

Be very kind to yourself. Seek wise counsel and support. Know you are not alone. Reject the words that minimise, or dismiss what you have been through. Find things that give you joy. Poet Zoe Snowden says:

"I have learnt that some pain can never entirely heal, only soften its jagged edges, so, it can nestle up comfortably to the joy in my heart." *Ref*
10.3

Advise the authorities if other children are in danger (you can do this anonymously – see resources page).

Know this is a wonderful life, as Psalm 91 verse 11 (NIV) assures us:

"He will command his angels concerning you, to guard you in all your ways."

References

10.1 Dern L, (Time's Up, 2018)

*10.1.1 * L Radford, etal, 'Child Abuse and Neglect in the UK Today' (London: NSPCC 2011)* www.nspcc.org

10.2 Lascelle GD (Breakthrough. The Art of Surviving, 2019)
www.traumabreakthrough.org

10.3 Snowden, Z. (@myjourneybackhome, Instagram, 2019)

10.4 Twigg, Stephen, MP, 2018, Chair of the International Development Committee (IDC) www. committees.parliament.uk

Resources and Contacts

Books and CD mentioned in this book or recommended by me:

The Book of Forgiving - The four-fold Path of healing for ourselves and our world by Desmond Tutu and Mpho Tutu, which includes a section on "Acknowledging the Harm". 2014 plus other books on forgiveness.

Father Forgive – The Forgotten F Word by Robin Oake. 2008.

Total Forgiveness - RT Kendall, 2001, updated 2020, RT Kendall Ministries

The Hiding Place by Corrie ten Boom. 1971.

Freedom in Christ course books by Neil T Anderson and Steve Goss (see www.ficm.org.uk) 2017.

From Report to Court A handbook for adult survivors of sexual violence. This Home Office funded report can be downloaded FREE from www.rightsofwomen.org.uk or www.rapecrisis.org.uk or a printed copy can be requested from the police.

The Body Keeps the Score: Brain, Mind and Body in Healing Trauma by Bessel Van der Kolk Child 2015.

Breakthrough; the Art of Surviving by Giles D. Lascelle 2019.

Success from the Inside Out by Nona Jones 2020 (a Zondervan title).

Insights into Helping Survivors of Childhood Sexual Abuse by Heather Churchill and Wendy Bray 2012 (CWR Waverley)

Inspiring Calm, and other CDs by John Mansfield, offering scriptural meditations.

CONTACTS UK (correct at time of publishing.):

Help for survivors of current and non-recent abuse. Many help friends and family too; some help perpetrators.	
If calling from outside the UK: From a landline dial 0044 before you dial the number. From a mobile dial +44 and lose the first 0 from the number	

Organisation	Contact
Association for People Abused in Childhood (NAPAC). Supporting recovery from child abuse	www.napac.org.uk 0808 801 0331
Association of Child Abuse Lawyers (ACAL). Legal support around child abuse	www.childabuselawyers.com
Association of Christian Counsellors (ACC).	www.acc-uk.org
Bible Gateway. Bible references	www.biblegateway.com
British Association for Counselling & Psychotherapy (BACP).	www.bacp.co.uk
Care for the Family Help building stronger families.	www.careforthefamily.org.uk 029 2081 0800
Childline. Help for/ around children's concerns	www.childline.org.uk 0800 1111
Citizen's Advice Bureau (CAB) Advice around Domestic abuse	www.citizensadvice.org.uk Look up local number

Children's Society. For children in England & Wales	www.childrenssociety.org.uk
Crimestoppers Anonymously report information	www.crimestoppers-uk.org 0800 555111
Criminal Injuries Compensation Authority (CICA). Govt body for compensation for victims of crime	www.gov.uk/government/organisations/criminal-injuries-compensation-authority
FindaChurch. Register of churches	www.findachurch.co.uk
Domestic abuse Perpetrator Programme (DVPP).	www.cafcass.gov.uk
Dot Com Children's Foundation. Empowering children	www.dotcomcf.org
Her Majesty's Prison & Probation Service. Oversees court sentences.	www.gov.uk/government/organisations/national-offender-management-service
Family Matters UK. Rape & Sexual Abuse Support Services	www.familymattersuk.org/isva 01474 536661
Faith & Freedom. Christian training - domestic abuse	www.faithandfreedom.webs.com
Freedom in Christ Ministries - identity and courses	www.ficm.org.uk
Forgiving.org. Effects on health	www.forgiving.org
Immanuel Approach Prayer Ministry	www.immanuelpracticum.com

Incest & Sexual Abuse Survivors (ISAS) Nottinghamshire. Self -refer for support	www.isas-notts.org.uk
Independent Inquiry into Child Sexual Abuse (IICSA). Statutory inquiry into failure to protect children from abuse	www.iicsa.org.uk 0800 917 1000
International Society for Traumatic Stress Studies (ISTSS). Traumatic stress science and research	www.istss.org
Lifeline. Support for those in distress or despair in Northern Ireland	www.lifelinehelpline.info 0808 8088000
Multi-Agency Safeguarding Hub (MASH). For raising concerns anonymously.	Search 'care, 'on local council website
Me Too Movement. Fighting sexual harassment & assault.	www.metoomvmt.org
MENding UK. For male survivors of sexual violation	www.mending-uk.org/ 01623 622916
Men's Advice Line For men experiencing domestic abuse	www.mensadviceline.org.uk 0808 801 0327
Minister & Clergy Sexual Abuse Survivors (MACSAS)- for those sexually abused by church workers etc.	www.macsas.org.uk 0808 8010340

NSPCC. Support for anyone worried about a child 24/7	www.nspcc.org.uk 0800 8005000
National Domestic Abuse Helpline. For women experiencing domestic abuse	www.nationaldomesticviolencehelpline.org.uk 0800 200 0247
National Rape Crisis. For victims of rape, child sex abuse or any sexual violence.	www.rapecrisis.org.uk 0808 802 9999
National Stalking Helpline. For those who fear they are being stalked	www.suzylamplugh.org 0808 802 0300
NHS Sexual Health Clinic Sexual health information and help	www.nhs.uk/oneyou/sexual-health 0300 123 7123 or 111
Notts Sexual Violence Support Services, Nottingham	www.nottssvss.org.uk 0115 9410440
Our Daily Bread. Christian resources	www.ourdailybread.org
PACE. Parents Against Child Sexual Exploitation	www.paceuk.info 0113 2405226
PODS. Positive Outcomes for Dissociative Survivors	www.pods-online.org.uk 0800 181 4420
Police. To report a crime or to get advice	www.police.uk. 999 in an emergency or 111 if not
Rape Crisis England & Wales. Support for those affected by sexual violence	www.rapecrisis.org.uk Local numbers or 0808 8029999

Rape Crisis, Scotland. Support for those affected by sexual violence	www.rapecrisisscotland.org.uk Local numbers or 0808 8010302
Refuge. Supporting survivors of abuse and domestic abuse	www.refuge.org.uk 0808 2000 247
Respect. Helping perpetrators to stop inflicting domestic abuse.	www.respect.uk.net 0808 802 4040
Restored. Christians ending violence against women.	www.restoredrelationships.org
Restorative Justice UK. Restorative training and services	www.remediuk.org
Rights of Women helping women through the law.	www.rightsofwomen.org.uk/get-advice/
Safeline. Support and counselling for male survivors of sexual abuse or rape	www.safeline.org.uk 0808 8005005
Safe Families for Children Supporting families in crisis.	www.safefamiliesforchildren.com
Samaritans 24/7. Listeners. You don't have to be suicidal	www.samaritans.org 116123
S.H.E. UK, Mansfield. Supporting survivors of abuse	www.she-uk.org.uk 01623 622916
SV2, Derbyshire. Supporting survivors of sexual violence	www.sv2.org.uk/ 01773 746115
STOP SO. Preventing sexual offences	www.stopso.org.uk

Survivors of Abuse (SOB). Mindset, nutrition & fitness	www.survivorsofabuse.org.uk
Survivors Trauma and Abuse Recovery Trust (START). For victims of abuse	www.start-online.org.uk 01480 878409
Survivors Trust. For survivors of rape, sexual abuse or child sexual abuse	www.thesurvivorstrust.org 0808 8010818
Survivors UK. Support and counselling for men and children survivors	www.survivorsuk.org . Web chat: counselling fee may apply.
TBN UK - Christian television broadcasters	www.tbnuk.org
The Rowan, Northern Ireland. Services for those who have been sexually abused, assaulted or raped	www.therowan.net 0800 3894424
Time's Up Movement. Safe & dignified work for women.	www.timesupnow.com
Topaz Centre. For survivors of rape & sexual assault- Nottingham & Notts	topazsupport@nottssvss.org.uk 0845 600 15 88
Truth Project. Sharing experiences.	www.truthproject.org.uk
United Christian Broadcasters	www.ucb.co.uk
The Victims' Commissioner - a voice for victims	www.victimscommissioner.org.uk
Victim Support, England & Wales 24/7 support after crime or trauma	www.victimsupport.org.uk 0808 1689111

Victim Support, Northern Ireland Support after crime or trauma	www.victimsupportni.co.uk 0208 90243133
Victim Support, Scotland 24/7 support after crime or trauma	www.victimsupportsco.org.uk 0345 6039213
Women's Aid. 24/7 Help for those experiencing domestic abuse	www.womensaid.org.uk 0808 2000
World Health Organization (WHO). International health in UN system	www.who.int

To ask Jesus into your life you can say a simple prayer such as:

Dear Lord Jesus, I believe you are the son of God. Please forgive me for living separately from you. Thank you for dying and overcoming death, to save me from my own wrong-doing, which I now turn away from. I invite you into my heart now and put my trust in you as I follow you in this life and into eternity. Amen.

I suggest reading your Bible, meeting Christians at your local church, looking up Christian resources; praying and listening for the Holy Spirit:

"Ask and it will be given to you; seek and you will find; knock and the door will be opened." Matthew 7 verse 7 (NIV).

"And we know that in all things God works for the good of those who love him, who have been called according to his purpose." Romans 8 verse 28.

My prayer for you, inspired by Psalm 143 verses 8-10:

Let the morning bring you word of God's unfailing love for you,

as you put your trust in him.

May he show you the way you should go

as you lift your soul to him.

O Lord, please rescue this person from any enemies,

as they draw near to you.

Teach them to do your will, for you are their God;

may your good spirit lead them on level ground.

From Psalm 37 (NIV):

"Turn from evil and do good; then you will dwell in the land forever.

For the Lord loves the just and will not forsake his faithful ones.

Commit your way to the Lord; trust in him and he will do this:

he will make your righteous reward shine like the dawn,

your vindication like the noonday sun."

Some encouragement from Romans 8 verse 37 (NIV):

"No, in all these things we are more than conquerors through him who loved us."

And abridged from Philippians 4 verse 8 (NIV):

"Finally, brothers and sisters, whatever is true … noble… right… pure … lovely

…admirable … excellent or praiseworthy – think about such things."

And a blessing from Numbers 6 verse 26 (NIV)

"… the Lord turn his face toward you and give you peace."